Teaching and Learning Basic Skills

*A Guide for Adult Basic Education
and Developmental Education Programs*

Teaching
and Learning
Basic Skills

A Guide for Adult Basic Education
and Developmental Education Programs

MARK H. ROSSMAN
Arizona State University

ELIZABETH C. FISK
Arizona State University

JANET E. ROEHL
University of Wisconsin–Stout

TEACHERS
COLLEGE
PRESS

Teachers College, Columbia University
New York and London   1984

Published by Teachers College Press, 1234 Amsterdam Avenue, New York, N.Y. 10027

Epigraph on page 3 is from "The Death of the Hired Man" from *The Poetry of Robert Frost,* edited by Edward Connery Lathem. Copyright 1930, 1939, © 1969 by Holt, Rinehart and Winston. Copyright © 1958 by Robert Frost. Copyright © 1967 by Lesley Frost Ballantine. Reprinted by permission of Holt, Rinehart and Winston, Publishers.

Library of Congress Cataloging in Publication Data

Rossman, Mark H., 1940–
  Teaching and learning basic skills.

  Bibliography: p.
  Includes index.
  1. Fundamental education—United States.
2. Elementary education of adults—United States.
I. Fisk, Elizabeth C. II. Roehl, Janet E., 1953–
III. Title.
LC5162.R67 1984   374'.012'0973   83-9118

ISBN 0-8077-2746-6

Manufactured in the United States of America

89 88 87 86 85 84   1 2 3 4 5 6

CONTENTS

PREFACE

Today there are countless adults in need of basic education. They are the millions who for a variety of reasons are unable to function at levels commensurate with their real abilities. They are a neglected and often overlooked population, who with only a limited ability in reading, writing, and numeracy are laboring simply to survive in our advanced, technological world. Historically, they have been served by a variety of educational programs. Literacy campaigns have been sponsored at local, national, and international levels and have been carried out by private, public, and volunteer groups. Despite the many efforts of these concerned groups, this population remains largely unserved.

In the United States there are two major providers of basic instruction in literacy and numeracy to adults: Adult Basic Education (ABE) programs, begun in the 1960s as part of the war on poverty and usually located in the public sector; and open-door community colleges through their growing "developmental education" programs. Despite obvious areas of overlap, the two types of programs frequently have had little interaction. Teachers, learners, program developers, and administrators rarely have spoken to one another. Successes, failures, and innovations in one program type have been virtually unknown in the other. Recently, as areas of commonality have become better known, this gap has begun to close. This book has been written to further bridge this gap by addressing concerns common to both ABE and developmental education.

Teaching and Learning Basic Skills is an aid to faculty and staff in both ABE and developmental education programs. It is appropriate for use in preservice and inservice staff or faculty development settings, as it contains relevant information regarding the clientele of both programs and addresses many of the common concerns of instructional personnel. Counselors, teacher-aides, and administrators will also find the material useful. Those preparing to enter the field of basic adult education through university coursework or degree programs often find that materials regarding programmatic concerns in this area are not available. This book provides the background information necessary to understand and appreciate the uniqueness of learning and teaching in this often-ignored area of higher and adult education.

Chapter 1 serves as an overview that describes the evolution of ABE and developmental education programs and outlines a number of key issues and objectives central to teaching basic skills to adults. The book then divides into two main parts: part 1 focuses on the nature of the adult learner in basic skills programs, and part 2 deals with the process of teaching.

Chapter 2 describes the learner in terms of physiological and psychological characteristics and discusses mental abilities and their effects on adult learning. Specific implications for the teacher are offered. Chapter 3 addresses a frequent concern related to the learner in basic skills programs—how to improve the self-concept.

Part 2 includes four chapters, each of which identifies a critical aspect of teaching for the basic skills instructor. Each chapter not only presents information but also provides application exercises. Each chapter is a discrete unit that may be used independently of the others.

Part 2 begins with chapter 4, which is concerned with the asking and answering of questions. This chapter looks at reasons for asking questions and provides techniques for asking and responding. Chapter 5 provides alternatives to traditional testing. The selection and design of appropriate test items, as well as options to paper-and-pencil tests, are provided. Chapter 6 responds to the need to simplify reading materials for basic skills students. It presents a method of assessing readability and suggests techniques for rewriting materials at reading levels appropriate for the adult learner. Chapter 7 is included because of the inadequacy many instructors feel in instructing the nonreader. It provides the opportunity to become familiar with four methods of teaching beginning reading. Through the use of a unique code alphabet, the instructor as reader will experience the frustration often associated with beginning to learn to read.

This book combines theory and practice with the authors' perspectives, which were developed as practitioners and administrators in adult basic education and developmental education programs in a variety of settings. Much of the material has been initially developed and field tested by the authors as part of a staff development project for the Adult Education Division of the Arizona Department of Education, Thus, it was designed and has been revised to reflect the specific concerns raised by practitioners themselves. It is hoped that this book will be one of many efforts dedicated to the needs of both ABE and developmental education programs.

ACKNOWLEDGMENTS

There are many individuals who have contributed to the development of this book. To list them all by name would make this section much too long. They know who they are and they have our deep-felt gratitude. They include the many Arizona adult basic education and developmental education teachers and administrators who read and critiqued the original version of this book. They also include the many graduate students from the Department of Higher and Adult Education at Arizona State University who similarly reviewed early manuscripts.

Particular thanks are given to the Arizona Department of Education, Adult Education Division, for providing funds through Title III, Section 309(c), P.L. 91-230 in support of the original two-volume work entitled *Adult Education Staff Development,* edited by Dr. Mark H. Rossman. It is from this work that the present book was devised. Special thanks must also go to Dr. Maxine Rossman for her contributions to chapter 2.

OVERVIEW

chapter 1

THE EVOLUTION
OF ADULT BASIC
EDUCATION
AND DEVELOPMENTAL
EDUCATION PROGRAMS

Nothing to look backward to with pride
Nothing to look forward to with hope ...
Robert Frost

In "The Death of the Hired Man," Frost has captured the sense of frustration, hopelessness, and despair that is the frequent companion of many undereducated and uneducated functionally illiterate adults. In the United States, the 1970 census revealed that more than 24 million adults (16 or older) in the labor force have less than a high school diploma. This equates to nearly one-quarter of the nation's entire labor force.

The lack of a formal education certificate is only part of the problem. In addition to job obsolescence, unemployment and frequent layoff, these adults have to cope with society's assumption that the unemployed and undereducated are lazy, shiftless, and lacking in self-respect. In addition, a poor self-image and a sense of hopelessness often contribute to the problems associated with adults who have academic deficiencies.

BASIC SKILLS PROGRAMS FOR ADULTS

For years, the responsibility for educating the adult illiterate has been perceived as the province of those involved in public school Adult Basic Education (ABE) programs. Historically, ABE has encompassed elementary education for adults, English as a Second Language (ESL), and preparation for the General Equivalency Diploma (GED) exam. Since 1964, the ABE program, funded under the Economic Opportunity Act of 1964 and its successor the Adult Education Act of 1966, has been a federally supported program operated through a system of grants to the various states and territories. Adults seeking basic skills, however, are also being serviced through the programs offered at community colleges, four-year colleges and universities, vocational schools, proprietary programs, military programs, and business and industry.

It is as difficult to establish the numbers of adults engaged in these educational efforts as it is to determine how many adults are in need of literacy acquisition. Historically, ABE programs have enrolled less than three percent of the total eligible population of 54 million adults listed as having less than a high school education. However, adults in need of this service permeate all educational strata. Roughly one-third of adult school enrollees are in adult basic education programs sponsored by the federal government. Even in institutions of higher education, an increasing percentage of students needs instruction in basic skills. At Pennsylvania State University, for example, 28 percent of entering students were described as lacking basic English skills (Hudspeth, 1978). Further, classes to boost literacy are frequently included as on-the-job training; since 1977, the number of basic education programs in business has doubled (Teft, 1982).

Providing basic adult education is one of the most challenging educational efforts a society can undertake. It requires commitment, coordination, and a sense of priority and urgency. The challenge is especially difficult because adults who need basic education are individuals who have not been well served by existing school systems. Meeting their needs requires creative, original approaches to program development and operation.

Many rationales directed at both society and the individual have been offered for basic adult education programs. From a societal perspective, basic education is justified as an investment that will bring economic and political returns. Universal literacy is believed to increase national prosperity and raise the standard of living. In some countries, it is linked to national strength and democratic potential. Such views, which undergird the massive literacy campaigns in developing Third World countries, are simplistic and often ignore the complex socioeconomic factors involved in achieving national prosperity.

Basic adult education is also justified on the basis of individual benefit. When adults improve their basic skills, they increase their opportunities for further education and employment. This can lead to social mobility and higher earning potential. They also increase self-confidence and self-esteem, the benefits of which are not readily quantifiable. Basic skills programs are necessary to fulfill the promises of equal opportunity policies begun in the 1960s. Recent efforts to promote equal access to higher education, occupational training, and job placement cannot succeed unless individuals are helped to acquire the communication and computation skills they will need to profit from these opportunities.

A related argument involves the expected benefit to the children of adult students. A strong relationship between home environment and academic achievement has been repeatedly demonstrated. There is also a direct relationship between participation in adult basic skills programs and the educational success of children. In this view, improvement in the educational potential of the next generation is insured by investing in the education of adults.

A somewhat different rationale, less tied to outcome measures, considers education as a basic human right. While the previous arguments viewed basic education as a calculated investment to be judged by its payoff to the individual and society, this position sees it as a good thing to be valued in and of itself. Every citizen should have the right to participate because that participation represents an improvement in the quality of their lives. In this view, developing communication and computation skills is a desirable goal regardless of whether it leads to economic or social advantage.

While the rhetoric of the 1960s involved outspoken expression of one or more of these arguments, the climate of the 1980s is more cautious. In economically troubled times, basic education is often given a low priority when spending decisions are made. At a time when basic education is most desperately needed, public support is decreasing. People seem to be skeptical regarding the wisdom of the rationales offered in support of it. Implicitly and explicitly they are saying that they do not believe society will benefit from an investment in basic adult education.

In light of fiscal restraints regarding educational programs, it has never been more important for advocates of basic adult education to become even more vociferous and for those involved in teaching and administrating such programs to further their knowledge and skills as providers and supporters of basic education for adults. Adult educators in local programs need to gain a wider perspective and greater appreciation of the various types of programs being offered across the country. By examining other adult skills training programs and their varying objectives, clienteles, and preferred methods of instruction, innovations or new ways to proceed may be discovered that enhance the quality and quantity of learning. Such interaction may help the instructor to more efficiently aid the student in the attainment of his goals.

Types of Programs

Basic education programs are offered by a variety of private, public, and voluntary agencies. Perhaps the most widespread programs are the state-administered programs funded by the federal government through the Adult Education Act of 1966 as amended, and those provided by community colleges through their developmental studies programs.

State-Administered Programs. ABE programs are provided throughout the country by local agencies, such as school districts and community centers, through federal funds administered by state departments of education. Government sponsorship of ABE began in the mid-1960s as part of the antipoverty program. Under the Economic Opportunity Act of 1964, a special title program was established to address the educational needs of adults lacking basic skills in reading and writing the English language. This program was expected to contribute to the achievement of economic self-sufficiency for the unskilled and undereducated segments of society. Monies were dispersed by the Department of Health, Education, and Welfare through grants to states. The states were to use the funds to facilitate local ABE programs and to stimulate the development of innovative methods and materials for instruction.

Since its inception, the ABE program has continually modified its administrative structure within the federal government to reflect the periodic reorganization of the Department of Education. Important changes have been made in the program's scope and emphasis. Originally aimed at those individuals 18 years of age and over who had completed less than six years of schooling, ABE has expanded its focus to include those 16 years of age and older (1968), to encompass preparation for a high school diploma (1969), and to involve all adults regardless of whether they have received a secondary school credential, if they lacked sufficient basic skills to function effectively in society (1978). Emphasis has been placed on serving special populations, including Native Americans (1972), older Americans (1973), bilingual and limited English-speaking adults (1974), Indochinese refugees (1976), and institutionalized adults (1978). Through the years, the federal leadership of ABE has attempted to facilitate the coordination of ABE programs with other social service agencies, the involvement of community members in program planning, and the availability of resources and staff development activities.

The expansion and changing emphasis in ABE reflects shifts in the social climate of the times as well as the rhetoric of each new federal administration. While few deny the contribution made by the locally based, federally funded programs, the ABE effort can be criticized because the commitment of resources, while substantial, has been inadequate in comparison with the idealistic expansion of program goals. With the widening scope, the original target population may have been slighted. Those adults with less than six years of formal schooling, who need the most basic help are, for many reasons, the hardest to reach and the most difficult to serve. Only the most concerted effort can hope to serve this "unreachable" population. The expanding focus of ABE has diluted the attention paid to them. While ABE programs are already overextended in their program goals, the current tightening of federal domestic spending makes the future of ABE uncertain.

Developmental Education.   Currently, basic education is also being offered to adults through developmental education programs at community colleges. The developmental education function of community colleges arose as a result of the "open-door" policies of the late 1960s. The promotion of open access to community colleges and many four-year colleges and universities led to a growing need for special education to help the large number of "new" (Cross, 1971) students admitted to higher education institutions who are unprepared to attempt college-level work. Realizing that without assistance the newly opened door to higher education would become a revolving door and that the promise of equal opportunity would be an empty one, colleges began to offer summer programs, special coursework, and tutorial services to assist this population.

Starting with a few courses in English, reading, and mathematics at the remedial level, insitutions soon developed a proliferation of such "zero-level" coursework. English 100, for example, was augmented by English 091, then English 028, 015, and so forth. Many colleges have now established separate divisions of developmental studies that attempt to coordinate the course offerings within and across subject areas.

As developmental education became a separate, recognized function of the community college, associations of developmental educators were formed, annual conferences held, and specialized journals published. The community college literature today includes frequent reference to the unique problems and potentials of this new area of programming.

Counseling services have become an important part of the new programs. ESL has increased in significance, especially in locations with large immigrant populations. As the scope of coursework has extended to include more and more fundamental levels of coursework, colleges have experimented with intensive, self-contained basic skills programs for the students most in need of basic education and skill training.

While the original philosophy of remedial courses had been preparation for regular college instructional programs, the evolving rationale for developmental education has not been tied to college participation. Idealistically expressed as taking students from "where they are to where they want to go," many of today's programs are designed to improve basic skills for more effective functioning in all aspects of daily life.

Although the same potential populations are being recruited by both ABE and developmental education programs, the college-based programs have remained quite distinct. In fact, the same college campus may house both programs. It is not uncommon to see a free ABE program offered on a Saturday morning and a developmental basic skills program offered as part of the regularly scheduled courses during the week. The students in the developmental education program will pay college fees and/or tuition. Most, if not all, will receive financial aid in the form of Pell Grants. They will be awarded college credit that, while not transferable, can often be used toward a modified associate of arts degree.

While some have advocated the community college as the preferred setting for basic skills instruction, especially in light of its more adult, collegiate atmosphere, problems arise when community colleges try to fulfill too many functions. This is especially true if the new developmental education program contrasts sharply with existing programs. Colleges may enthusiastically take on a role for which they do not have the necessary resources and expertise. Whatever the sponsoring agency or the institutional setting, however, effective basic adult education requires a careful assignment of resources and gathering of expertise that is guided by clearly defined objectives.

Objectives

The objectives of basic education programs have changed with evolving conceptions of what constitutes literacy. Often objectives have been linked with the communication and computation skills included in the formal elementary school curriculum. The clientele are considered as those "off-time" individuals who did not acquire the skills usually taught in public schools. Thus, the program is designed to give these individuals the opportunity to return and acquire the skills they missed. The focus is on the reading and arithmetic skills associated with the primary school classroom.

More recently, there has been a trend toward objectives associated with a more functional view of literacy. The content, as well as the materials and methods of instruction, have been designed to be more appropriate for adults. As part of the movement toward "competency-based education," functional literacy involves the identification and development of those communication and computation skills that adults need for work, home, and community life.

In addition, there has been a realization that a complex set of skills is required in even the most basic levels of communication and computation. Becoming functionally literate involves the development of perceptual and cognitive skills, and a familiarity with "written dialects" that use unique vocabulary and sentence structures. Functional literacy also requires the acquisition of new concepts and cultural awarenesses as students come into contact with new contexts for communication and thought.

The decision to participate in basic education also represents an experience that can profoundly affect adults' self-concepts and challenge longstanding attitudes toward their lives and their worlds. For this reason, basic skills programs need to include objectives designed to help students take full advantage of the positive potential in the change process inherent in a basic education.

While the increasing breadth of objectives reflects a more realistic picture of the complex learning involved in basic skills education, there is a danger that programs will become too diffuse. In trying to meet all the needs of their students, they may meet none of them well.

Clientele

The potential and actual clientele for basic adult education include a number of overlapping subgroups, each of which need somewhat different educational services:

- Individuals who never had the opportunity to acquire basic skills, although they may have been successful in other aspects of life.
- Individuals who have met repeated failures in learning and in other areas of life. Poor and unemployed, they may have developed a defeatist attitude and a poor self-concept.
- Individuals who have a learning disability in the area of basic reading and computation.
- Culturally distinct individuals for whom the educational programs of the dominant culture have been inappropriate.
- Immigrants well educated in their own countries who need to learn the language and sociocultural norms of this country.
- Immigrants with little or no education whose need to learn English is complicated by their unfamiliarity with formal instructional settings and procedures.

Problems arise when programs do not clearly identify the differing subgroups represented among their students. They may be attempting to serve students with radically different needs within the same program, and the individuals who come to make up their clientele may not be those for whom the program was originally intended to serve.

Instructional Methods

A variety of instructional methods has been utilized in basic education programs. Programs emphasizing oral language competence for second-language speakers rely heavily on small group drills and conversation practice. Programs for beginning readers prefer one-to-one tutoring, while more comprehensive basic skills programs for native speakers have shown a trend toward individualized instruction. Individualization is deemed necessary in adapting to the diversity of students and inconsistencies in attendance. It is also believed to foster self-directed learning. However, individualized programs are difficult to design and implement well and require special training and support for instructors. Students, too, need assistance in adjusting to the responsibility and solitary experience of working on their own.

Whatever the instructional approach or approaches used, materials are needed that are appropriate in content and style for adults and flexible enough in format to allow instructors to adapt and individualize them for their students and their teaching situation. In all programs, there is a need to schedule instruction that takes into account both the exigencies of the students' lives and the requirements of effective learning. Often, for both internal and external reasons, students are not able to participate often enough to promote effective learning or at times when they are most able to profit from instruction.

Issues

A number of important issues must be faced if basic education programs are to survive and increase. All providers of basic skills education must coordinate their efforts in terms of planning, recruitment, and resource allocation. In addition, they need to explore the relationships among their programs and (1) the formal educational system of elementary, secondary, and higher education; (2) vocational preparation programs: and (3) the wide variety of continuing educational services for adults.

Further, connections should be strengthened among educational programs and other services within a broadly conceived economic and social policy. Improvement in basic skills can have an impact on the lives of adults only if it comes as part of a well-articulated effort to improve individual and social welfare.

The past experiences of adult educators provide a wealth of valuable information for program planners and instructors. While coordination and communication networks have been increasing, there is a need to improve the availability of information about the nature and consequences of varying approaches to instruction and program operation.

In order to move toward more effective programming, thorough evaluation is needed of both individual student progress and program effectiveness and efficiency. Evaluation efforts, if they are to be more than paper-shuffling exercises, should supply the types of data that will be most useful to students, instructors, and policymakers. The data should include direct measures of the competencies gained by students, not just the numbers who have passed through the programs. Decisions have to be made as to which measures are most important to describe and what extent of progress constitutes a significant improvement. There is also a need for follow-up studies of students after they finish programs to better see the long-term impact of participation on multiple aspects of the students' lives. In addition to outcome measures, program planners need ongoing information on all aspects of their programs.

The type of evaluative effort recommended here is costly in terms of dollars, time, and effort. With minimum funds available for program operation, it is difficult to make a decision to invest scarce resources in the sort of evaluation that is really needed. Instead, evaluations often become hasty presentations of surface level data that reveal little about the realities of the program.

However, the information that has been shared makes it increasingly obvious that programs must take into account cultural, geographic, and linguistic factors and the needs of special populations. The answers to questions about instructional objectives and methods are becoming increasingly variable, situation-specific, and complex.

In the face of this complexity, staff development becomes the key to progress. Instructors and administrators dedicated to providing basic education to adults need to continually increase their skill in articulating purposes and goals, utilizing effective teaching techniques, and, most especially, adapting to the characteristics, motivations, and needs of their students.

Part I

THE LEARNER IN ABE
AND DEVELOPMENTAL
EDUCATION PROGRAMS

chapter 2

THE NATURE
OF THE LEARNER

Probably the most important responsibility for those working with under-educated or uneducated adults in any setting is to understand the nature of those with whom they are working. As many of the instructors of this population are young and have not personally experienced the aging process and its effects on learning, it is important that the aging process be understood. Implicit is the underlying assumption that teachers, in order to do their job, must have this knowledge in order to effectively perform their task. Without knowledge of the adult learner at various ages even the most competent instructor cannot be expected to be fully effective.

In order to provide this information, this chapter is divided into three sections: (a) physiological and (b) psychological changes in the adult learner, and (c) mental abilities of the adult and their effect on adult learning. Each section concludes with implications for the adult educator.

PHYSIOLOGICAL FACTORS

Vision

Adults with normal good health depend more upon vision in learning than upon any other sense. It is estimated that 85 percent of all learning occurs through vision. Although the life span of the eye exceeds life expectancy, there is a steady decrease in the average efficiency of the eye with advancing age, even in otherwise healthy eyes. The percentage of the pop-

ulation with defective vision shows a sharp increase from 23 percent at age
20 to 95 percent at age 70 (Verner & Davison, 1971).

Visual Acuity. The primary measurement that reflects the efficiency
of vision is the measurement of visual acuity. Studies have indicated that
visual acuity attains its maximum at about 18 to 20 years of age. The near-
point of vision (the distance from the eye at which an object can be seen
clearly) begins to move away from the eye after 10 years of age. The most
striking change occurs between 45 and 55 years of age. The decrease in
vision after, or at least beginning at, age 40 appears to reflect changes in
at least four factors: pupil diameter, ability to adapt to the dark, sensitivity
to glare, and yellowing of the lens (Bischof, 1976, pp. 104–05).

Pupil Diameter. The size of the pupil tends to get smaller with age,
thus reducing the amount of light reaching the retina. Perhaps the most
sensitive indicator of the efficiency of the visual system is shown by the
minimum light threshold of the fully dark-adapted eye.

Dark Adaptation. Dark adaptation is the increase in visual sensitivity that occurs after remaining in the dark. It has been repeatedly demonstrated that the dark-adaptation threshold increases with age.

Illumination. It is possible to compensate for the changes in pupil
size by increasing the amount of light. For a normal learning task an adult
at age 20 requires 100 watts of illumination, but by age 50, 180 watts are
required for the same task to compensate for pupillary changes (Verner
and Davison, 1971).
     The ability of the eye to respond to a visual stimulus is also affected
by the aging process. Thus, not only is more light needed to compensate
for pupillary changes, it is also needed to compensate for the decrease in
visual recognition that accompanies the natural aging process.

Contrast. Another important aspect of illumination is the matter of
contrast. The learning task or stimulus must be set apart from its background so that it stands out as separate and distinct from its surroundings.
Contrast has a pronounced effect upon the speed of reading, which is
reduced significantly when the words being read are not in sharp contrast

with the paper on which they appear. There is also evidence showing that contrast sensitivity declines with age.

The ability of the eye to see clearly objects both far and near begins to decrease at about age six and constantly decreases until about age 60, after which it levels off until extreme old age. This occurs due to loss of elasticity of the lenses of the eye, causing the older lens to have a more fixed focus and reduced ability to adjust to objects close to the eye.

Color Vision.   There are some definite changes due to age insofar as color vision is concerned. After age 35, more blue light is needed to get a sensation of blue. This loss of yellow-blue discrimination diminishes as one moves toward the red end of the spectrum. Thus, after age 35, learning tasks involving color will need to use strong rather than subtle tints.

Hearing

In no capacity except sight are there greater changes at different stages in life than in hearing. In most people the peak of performance seems to be reached before the fifteenth birthday, and there is gradual but consistent decline until about 65.

In addition to the loss of hearing efficiency as one ages, there is also a slowing of the central hearing processes. Individuals respond less quickly to auditory stimuli as they age. For this reason many older individuals find it difficult to follow rapid speech despite little or no hearing loss.

The prevalence of impaired hearing is quite marked at the upper age levels. Studies have demonstrated that the average hearing loss shows a marked increase past age 45 and continues to increase rapidly thereafter.

Sound Frequencies.   Hearing loss due to aging is not equal across all frequencies of sound. It appears that most individuals above age 40 will show some loss of high-tone perception, and there is a somewhat greater tendency for men to show impaired hearing than for women.

Discrimination.   The normal process of aging produces hearing loss due to changes in the ear that result in reduced ability to discriminate among sounds, causing impairment in speech discrimination. As one ages, it becomes increasingly more difficult to differentiate the sounds of the letters *v, d, b,* or *p.* Between ages 25 and 55 hearing discrimination decreases slightly, but after 55 the loss is more dramatic. To compensate for normal hearing loss in an adult learning situation, it is important for the instructor to speak slowly, distinctly, and with sufficient volume. Since hearing loss reduces one's ability to recall long sentences, an instructor should use short sentences—especially when giving directions for learning. This is particularly important when dealing with individuals suffering a hearing loss, as the inability to hear can produce emotional anxieties, such as fear and insecurity. Thus, in turn, an inability to hear can interfere with learning on both a physical and emotional level. As many ABE and developmental education program students already have a poor self-concept when they enter the program, it is particularly important that the instructor do everything possible to avoid adding to this problem.

Reaction Time

In addition to losses in vision and hearing, an additional effect of the aging process in the absence of disease is a slowing of reaction time. Since 1884, with the data collected by Galton, reaction speed has been found to increase from early childhood, reach its maximum at about 18 years of age, and then significantly decline beyond the forties. This phenomenon has been confirmed many times.

Emotional Reactions

At the same time that performance is being altered by the aging process, the adult is also being affected by the emotional response to physiological change. Consequently, physical changes often are accentuated by the emotional state they induce. As adults become less confident of their own abilities, they may take longer to perform familiar tasks than their physiological state alone would require. Some adults respond to a decrease in ability to perform efficiently by increased motivation and determination to overcome the loss, while others become depressed and discouraged to the point that their performance falls far below the potential of their actual physical state. In ABE and developmental education programs, it is not unusual for adult students with this type of concern to withdraw from the program without discussing the problem, thus perpetuating the myth that "I am too old to learn."

Instructional Implications of Physiological Changes

The teacher in ABE and developmental education settings has unique opportunities and challenges. It is obvious that the adult is not simply a tall, grown-up child. Physiologically, the adult is different from the child or youth in many ways and demands distinctly different actions on the part of the teacher. Some suggested procedures are as follows.

1. Use good illumination. Older adults must have not only better light, they must have more light. Do not have the audience face the light. Never have a flickering light.
2. Arrange seating so that people are close to the speaker and to the materials used in class demonstrations.
3. Arrange and use equipment that will enable the audience to see all parts of demonstrations easily and clearly. In addition:
    a. Have a neutral background.
    b. Use sharp contrast of color.
    c. Use large charts, diagrams, and pictures.
    d. Use large, legible letters when writing or printing on chalk-boards or flipcharts.
    e. Use simple words and phrases on the board. Avoid the use of abbreviations.
    f. Remove everything from the chalkboard except those items that pertain to the subject under discussion. This will assist the learner to focus on what is being written.
4. Shiny slate blackboards should be replaced wherever possible with the new, rough chalkboards of such color that maximum contrast can be obtained with selected chalk.
5. Wash the board when finished to remove chalk dust. This reduces problems associated with glare and contrast.
6. Make sure that all duplicated materials for student use are done with pica type and double spacing.
7. Speak more slowly and distinctly as the age of the group increases.
8. Stand still, or relatively so, so that those who depend to some extent, consciously or unconsciously, on lipreading will be aided in understanding what is being said.
9. Unusual words, unfamiliar names, numbers, and the like should be enunciated clearly and then printed on the chalkboard.

10. Study the faces of members of the group to see whether they are hearing.
11. Use simple, well-chosen words that are clear and meaningful; avoid the use of words that are lengthy and difficult to understand.
12. Use the chalkboard freely, particularly when there are some who are not hearing clearly; vision will supplement a hearing loss.
13. Talk directly to the group in a friendly, conversational manner; use a well-modulated voice; avoid monotone.
14. Be especially observant to eliminate inside or outside noises that tend to interfere with the hearing of the group.
15. Questions directed to the teacher by members of the group should be repeated for the benefit of the entire group before the questions are answered. (See chapter 4 for greater elaboration on this notion.)
16. Ask someone at the back of the room to get your attention when you are talking too softly, rapidly, or slowly.
17. Suggest that hearing and vision checkups become a regular part of the student's program.

PSYCHOLOGICAL FACTORS

Adult Life Stages

Only very recently have we come to study adults and adulthood as a developmental period in itself—a time during which maturation, accumulated experience, and learning serve to shape an age group that is distinct from childhood, adolescence, or extreme old age. This view is prevalent throughout the research in adult education. As Havighurst and Orr (1956, p. 1) concluded, "People do not launch themselves into adulthood with the momentum of their childhood and simply coast along to old age ... adulthood has its transition points and its crises.... It is a developmental period in almost as complete a sense as childhood and adolescence are developmental periods."

The developmental tasks an individual must learn are those that constitute healthy and satisfactory growth in our society. A developmental task arises at an appropriate period in the life of the individual. Successful achievement leads to happiness and to success with future tasks, while failure leads to difficulty with later tasks.

Whereas the developmental tasks of youth tend to be the products of physiological and mental maturation, those of the adult years are the products primarily of the evolution of social roles. Havighurst (1972) divides the adult years into three phases: early adulthood, middle age, and later maturity. Accordingly, the requirements for performing social roles change as the individual moves thorugh the three phases of adult life, thereby setting up changing developmental tasks and, therefore, changing readiness to learn.

With few exceptions, dynamic theories of personality have not been primarily concerned with the problems of change in adulthood, although Fromm (1941), Maslow (1954), and Jung (1933) have indicated that profound behavioral changes may occur during this time.

The adult personality is continuous but not identical with the personality of the child and the adolescent. The heightened importance of introspection in the mental life of middle-aged people (i.e., stock-taking, increased reflection, and the structuring and restructuring of experience) is vital. There is also a general movement of energy from an outer-world to an inner-world orientation. While it may not be true that life begins at 40, it seems indeed to be true that life is different after 40.

An awareness of psychological theories and needs in the life cycle is a critical factor for those working with adults. This awareness of the developmental stages, turning points, issues, and crises of adulthood will greatly enhance one's effectiveness in dealing with the adult learner at any level, but it is especially important when working with adults whose academic preparation is less than complete.

Perception of Time

One of the psychological processes that occurs in the middle years of life and promotes change in personality is the reevaluation of time. Adults are distinguished from youth and children by the ways in which they view time. The major events of life can be expected to occur in the 50 or more years of adult life. To be aware that one is behind, on, or ahead of schedule of life expectations can have a profound effect on life adjustment. It has been said that to the child the future is vague but just ahead, to the adolescent vague but unlimited. Adults, however, have a realistic attitude toward time that sharply differentiates their perspective from the outlook of youth.

The perception of time within the total life span may also influence the perspective of adults. Some sublimits may be biologically determined. For example, time is a crucial matter for the woman who marries late and wants children, or for the professional athlete seeking world records before becoming too old. Other time pressures are culturally determined, such as those felt by the entry-level clerk of 45 who aspires to be company president by age 55.

Another unique aspect of the adult years is the universal experience that time seems to pass faster as one grows older. For a youngster of six, one year is one-sixth of life. For a youth of 16, a year is one-sixteenth of that life. For an adult of 40, a year is one-fortieth, and at 70, merely one-seventieth of the years lived.

For an adult the investment of time in an activity may be as important a decision as the investment of money or effort. For this reason, most adult learners feel cheated if their time is wasted by the instructor. Since time is a valuable commodity, the instructor needs to give careful consideration to such concerns as homework, scheduling additional class periods, and field trips. Sensitivity to the time factor may be one of the most distinctive features in the psychology of the adult years.

Motivation

Time is a key influence on motivation. The adolescent is frequently viewed as having all the time in the world. Nothing seems impossible. But the woman of 45 and the man of 50 now realize that it may already be too late for the expression of some deeply felt needs and that all future objectives will depend upon how much time is left for their expression. The intensity of motives may deepen or lessen; a person may be determined to finish some task before it is too late or become resigned to the likelihood that it will never be finished.

Among middle-class Americans career drives are likely to take precedence over many other psychological needs and dominate the years of young adulthood, perhaps resulting in minimal contact with family. If by 40 or 45 the career-oriented individual has achieved economic security and success, the need to get ahead may be much less in evidence and this individual may turn to the family or to community activities as a source of gratification.

While motivation is extremely complex and not fully understood, it is best seen within the framework of an adult's needs, goals, habits, values, and self-concept. An adult's willingness to engage in learning depends upon such factors as the perception of the value of learning, the acceptance of what and how to learn, the need for self-esteem or social affiliation with others, and expectations from life.

Although there are many different notions about motivation and its influence upon learning, it can be concluded that intrinsic motivation is far more important than extrinsic motivation, especially when dealing with adults. Adults will generally be more motivated if the facilitator assists the learner to recognize the personal value of the material being presented.

Adult learners usually enter a learning center with a high degree of readiness to learn. The adult wants answers that are practical and relevant. The adult will most likely equate what they have learned to life experiences, make judgments, and use life experiences to make new decisions regarding the value of the learning experience. If adults see that relevant knowledge can be gained from activities in ABE or developmental education programs, they will more likely participate. If not, they will drop out. The fact that the adult learner is different makes the understanding of what Havighurst calls the "teachable moment" so important. That moment comes when a person has need for a skill or knowledge that will help solve a life problem.

Adult students are not always interested in total involvement in each instructional situation in which they take part. Rather, they are inclined to distribute their energies according to the kind and amounts of learning they feel would be most beneficial to them presently and in the future. While it is important to attempt to include the functionally illiterate adult in the learning transaction, it is important to also remember that this individual may not want to become totally involved. The responsibility of the instructor in this situation is to facilitate the needs of the learner.

Experience has shown that adults have more emotional associations with factual material than do children, although we usually assume they have less because the devices of control are more elaborate and better covered in the adult. This emotional association with words or events may affect the adult in gaining new knowledge.

Adults learn best the things that are in keeping with their value systems and their personal biases. It is important for the instructors to present information and discuss it in a way that is relevant to the learner.

Reasons for Attending

Another aspect of the relationship between learning and motives is seen in the reasons adults attend programs. In an in-depth study of 22 participants in adult education activities, Houle (1961) investigated their purposes and objectives. He classified the continuing learner as: (a) goal-oriented, those pursuing their education as a means of accomplishing fairly clear-cut objectives; (b) activity-oriented, those who take part in learning for reasons unrelated to the expressed purpose of the educational activity; and (c) learning-oriented, those seeking "learning for learning's sake." Learners generally identify with one category, but such factors as time of day, subject, or teacher may cause a change in the learners' orientations. They may shift from one category to another several times during the course of a learning experience. It is therefore impossible to classify the adult learner as *always* being "goal," "activity," or "knowledge" oriented.

Self-Concept

When adults participate in educational activities, they are especially concerned with maintaining and enhancing their social worth and success. Adults have a strong need to gain new knowledge and skills in an instructional situation, but only when there is no danger of losing hard-won prestige.

Adults even more than children are sensitive to failure in their learning situation, and their previous unfavorable experiences with education may cause fear and self-doubts about ability. There is some evidence to suggest that the fear of aging, rather than the aging process itself, may cause mental deterioration. This is particularly true for many adult learners in basic education programs.

Adult learners are more bound to stereotypes than are children. This follows through in almost every attitude, belief, and set of values. It is more difficult for adults to set these stereotypes aside and entertain conflicting, opposing points of view.

Even the way a person organizes perceptions, as well as what one selects to perceive, is influenced by individual expectations. These expectations depend on personal experience and motive. It is more difficult to change the perceptions of an adult than those of a child because the adult has had more prior experience.

Instructional Implications of Psychological Changes

Change and consistency in adult personality constitute a problem area that has attracted relatively few psychologists; nevertheless, evidence is beginning to accumulate that systematic and measurable shifts occur in the second half of life. Adults change through the years in sense of time, career patterns, physiological conditions, and complexity of interests and motivations. An understanding of adult psychology is a necessity for working with ABE and developmental education students, and the following are offered as guidelines:

To reduce the "anxieties" that many basic skills learners have:
1. Use an informal, friendly approach in greeting and working with all adults.
2. Present an accurate picture of what the learner should expect to gain and the purpose of the program.
3. Discuss the physical setting, including locations of restrooms, exits, snack bar, telephone, parking, etc.

To encourage a feeling of caring and being concerned:
4. Encourage the students to become acquainted with each other by introducing everyone at the opening session as well as introducing each new member added to the group.
5. Involve new students in the learning process as quickly and painlessly as possible.
6. Use positive reinforcement frequently, yet sincerely.
7. Insure that learning materials are consistent with ability level.

To more fully develop a sense of "self-worth":
8. Include each adult in the identification and clarification of specific goals and objectives.
9. Point out when and how progress is being made.
10. Acknowledge completion of a goal, objective, or task, particularly as it relates to those identified by the learner.
11. Encourage the sharing of successes with other members of the class.

MENTAL ABILITIES AND THEIR EFFECT ON ADULT LEARNING

The first part of this section contains four major areas bearing on the adult years: decline versus growth in intellectual functioning; speed versus power as a measure of intellectual ability; the changing patterns of mental abilities with increasing age; and the relationship between education and intellectual ability. It is followed by a discussion of implications for ABE and developmental education practitioners.

Decline Versus Growth

Most intelligence tests and measures of intellectual ability in adults have been adapted from those used with children or young adults. Implicit in the use of intelligence tests based on those of children is the notion that intelligence is related to school achievement. This is not a satisfactory standard for adults. A number of criteria might be posed to test the validity of the instruments of adult intelligence. Measures of intellectual function might be related to: (1) longevity; (2) occupation; (3) susceptibility to certain diseases, like cardiovascular disease; and (4) personality. It is also important to consider sex differences in relation to development of the intellect. Further, successful adult performance on intelligence tests calls for motivation, persistence in the task, cooperation with the psychometrist, and familiarity with the test items.

Intellectual Functioning. A significant problem with measuring adult intelligence is the degree to which data has been obtained from cross-sectional studies—those that evaluate change by comparing different adults representing different stages of development at the same point in time—and longitudinal studies—those that evaluate change by studying the same adults over various periods of time. Much conflicting information has been generated by these methods. However, certain patterns are emerging from the research. For example, longitudinal studies do not support the notion that intellectual functioning declines with advancing years. In fact, the opposite appears to be true. Many researchers now feel that an individual's pattern of living seems to be a major force in determining adult intelligence, particularly as it relates to life span. Research also seems to indicate that age, in and of itself, has little effect on an otherwise healthy individual's ability to learn or think.

Speed Versus Power

Thorndike et al. (1928) conducted comprehensive studies of adult learning and reported that changes take place in the amount and nature of the ability to learn from about age 15 to about age 45, particularly from age 25 to age 45. They conducted three extensive series of experiments, each including 200 or more learners and covering long periods of learning. The first concerned learning to read, write, and compute and covered a range of intellect from near average to very low levels. The second addressed the learning of typical high school subjects such as algebra, English, civics, and biology with adults ranging in intellect from near average to very high levels. The third dealt with learning typewriting and stenography with persons with a range of intellect from near average to very high levels of functioning. Intensive experiments in learning to write with the wrong hand, to typewrite, and to understand the artificial language, Esperanto, were also conducted.

The results of these experiments showed that: (a) on the average individuals probably learn much less per year from age 25 to 45 than they did from age 5 to 25; (b) the decline form the acme of ability to learn (probably between ages 20 and 25) to about 42 is only about 13 percent to 15 percent for a representative group of abilities; and (c) the influence of the intellect upon the curve of ability to learn in relation to age is slight.

Based on these data, Thorndike and his colleagues drew the following conclusions: (a) in general, nobody under 45 should restrain himself from trying to learn anything because of a belief or fear that he is too old to be able to learn; and (b) age, in itself, is a minor factor in either success or failure. Capacity, interest, energy, and time are the essentials. In their use of the concept of "amount per hour," they clearly distinguish between learning rate as efficiency or performance and learning ability as power or potential.

A problem with the Thorndike research is that it is based upon tests that stress and emphasize speed of response. If, as previously suggested, decrements in speed, vision, and hearing do characterize aging, then the evaluation of learning ability and intelligence needs to consider these abilities and not in terms of losses in performance.

In order to determine the relationship between age and various tests of mental ability, Lorge (1936) administered tests to 143 adults grouped as follows: (1) between 20 and 25 years, (2) between 27.5 and 37.5 years, and (3) between 40 and 70 years. Five intelligence tests, all timed, and one test of intellectual power with no time limitations were administered. On the timed tests the scores of the two older groups were, respectively, 15 to 25 percent below those of the youngest. However, on the untimed test, the scores were almost identical with less than 0.1 percent difference between the groups.

In the conclusion to this study, Lorge maintained that mixing power with speed measurements among older students obscures the true relationship of intellectual power to age. It is clear that learning ability does not significantly change from the early twenties through later life. Capable individuals in their early twenties do not suddenly become dull or obtuse in their later years. Similarly, it is impossible for one with limited ability to become an overachiever in the later years.

Pattern of Mental Abilities

As more refined intelligence tests became available, researchers began to realize that different intellectual measures might provide different results. For example, Eichorn (1973), using the Wechsler-Bellevue and *WAIS* tests administered to members in the Berkeley growth study, found that the subtests that maintain or increase with age are "vocabulary" and "information." Both subtests showed gains for both sexes through age 36.

Other studies reported that scores on perceptual and dexterity tests decline from the teens to the seventies, whereas other test scores for verbal fluency and comprehension showed no decline through the mid-forties. Interestingly, the decline in speed on motor tasks begins between the ages of 18 and 40, at a time when verbal scores are still increasing.

Since verbal abilities do not appear to decline with advancing age, one might expect little decline in the ability to receive verbal information. This assumption is not always correct. Rossiter (1970) conducted a study to determine the relationship between listening ability and chronological age. The subjects in the study were 30 female, upper-level undergraduate and graduate students at Ohio University during 1968. The ages ranged from 20 to 60 years. The significant relationship found between age and listening scores indicated that listening ability does decline with increased aging. It is suggested, therefore, that those teaching classes in which adult students may vary widely in age might be aware that older students may be retaining less from oral presentations than younger students.

The relative amount of knowledge in different academic subjects changes as a function of age. There is a progressive improvement in achievement in the humanities, social sciences, and history and a general decline in mathematics and the natural sciences. This classic adult pattern regarding verbal and performance scores has been demonstrated many times and now constitutes one of the best replicated results in the literature.

Education and Mental Ability

Many of the observed age differences in performance on learning tasks result from differences in experience and education. There is evidence to support the theory that inactivity in learning, rather than age, is related to the lower learning ability of some older adults. Sorenson (1930) indicated that there was no decline in learning ability for those who had recently participated in course work. There was, however, a slight decline in learning ability with age for those who had not recently participated. As many adult students in ABE and developmental education programs have never participated in formal courses, this situation is even more of a concern.

The adult's level of education as well as the recency of participation in an educational activity appear to be related to the ability to learn. The recent participant will frequently have a broader background knowledge and will usually have a clearer understanding of such intangibles as instructor style and personal learning objectives. In general, they will better know how to learn.

Most of what is known about adult learning has been taken from studies of learning in children and animals. Most of what is known about motivation has been derived from experience with teaching children under compulsory attendance regulations. Many instructors who are currently employed, as well as those now being trained, are not prepared to teach adults, as they have not been provided with appropriate information about biological, psychological, and sociological aspects of life-span development. This is equally true for those working in ABE and developmental education programs.

When adult education began to emerge as a field of social practice, it simply borrowed the assumptions and strategies of pedagogy. But when a falling retention rate in adult classes was noted, teachers began experimenting with different assumptions and strategies, and there began to emerge a body of literature describing successful teaching for adults.

Andragogy.   In the early 1960s European adult educators, especially in France, Germany, Yugoslavia, and the Netherlands, started using the label "andragogy" to identify this body of theory and technology of adult learning that stressed differing learning orientations and assumptions for children and adults. A description of andragogy as currently practiced might be the art and science of helping maturing individuals to learn.

Experiences.   Having lived longer and having a greater amount of past experience, adults are not only much more complex than children, they are also more differentiated and less dependent on immediate influences of the environment.

Kidd (1973) indicates three basic ways in which adulthood differs from youth: (1) adults have *more* experiences; (2) adults have *different kinds* of experiences; and (3) the life experiences of adults are *organized* differently.

Adults' experiences are different from those of children. It is unfortunate that this point has not always been understood or accepted. For example, an adult brings to the ABE program a tremendous range of stored learning, the accumulations from experiences in everyday living. These are a most important resource for learning.

On the other hand, in the case of many adults, long experience will cause them to be set in their ways and resentful of change. The more experience a person has had, the more the past probably will interfere with the present. It is easier for an experienced person to learn a completely new task than to learn to do a familiar task in a new way.

Nevertheless, the more the teacher of adults can base teaching upon the previous experiences of the learner, the better and faster the adult will learn. The teacher should urge adult learners to relate new or difficult concepts to their own experiences and to use the past to help understand the present and the future.

Learning Orientation.   Adults, even more than children, bring attitudes with them into the learning situation that can seemingly affect their ability to learn. Adults with feelings of powerlessness may fail to learn to control relevant information. They will be more motivated to listen and to read material that may increase their competence in a current situation.

Adult learners want educational experiences or knowlege that is related to job/life situations. They are more interested in applied knowledge than in theory, and they enter into a learning situation in a problem-centered frame of mind.

This change in orientation from subject-centeredness to problem-centeredness supports the contention stated earlier that adult students are not always interested in becoming involved in each instructional situation in which they take part. Rather, they are inclined to distribute their energy and involvement according to the kind and amount of learning they feel would be most beneficial now and in the future. The learner may be only concerned in learning how to compute the sales tax and not interested in knowing more about fractions or decimals. Students should be able to influence their own learning goals and make certain that these goals take account of their needs and problems. Since adults have compelling responsibilities competing for their time and attention, many adults desire minimal time requirements to complete their education objectives.

Learning Environments.   Adults usually learn more effectively and quickly in a noncompetitive atmosphere where they can collaborate with others and foster their own learning. Competition is a factor in raising anxiety levels. When compounded by the learner's existing anxiety level, the tension created by class competition, especially under a formal grading system, may result in an undesirable situation.

According to Knowles (1980, p. 49), "Nothing makes an adult feel more childlike than being judged by another adult; it is the ultimate sign of disrespect and dependency, as the one who is being judged experiences it." Evaluation, as all other phases of the adult learning experience, should be a mutual undertaking.

The threat of evaluation, such as objective tests graded on a competitive basis, probably should be avoided for adults. Teachers of adults should work to develop mutually acceptable criteria and methods for measuring progress, thereby helping the learner to develop and apply procedures for self-assessment according to these criteria. Involving the learners in selecting objectives enhances motivation and learning. Specific objectives should be stated in measurable terms to help the teacher effectively design the instruction and to facilitate measuring learning outcomes.

Too few teachers know enough about the adult learner's anxiety level. Many adults come to classes with a good deal of insecurity and anxiety about their ability to succeed in a new learning situation. Some of the most frequent suggestions for reducing anxiety are refresher courses and help in learning how to study.

Coming from a world of work where mistakes are costly, most adults have higher standards of performance than do children or youth; therefore, they have a strong need for the acquisition of knowledge and skills in an instructional situation in which there is no danger of losing hard-won prestige. Indeed, adults learn more effectively when they receive feedback regarding how well they are progressing. Punishment and threatening instructors slow up the learning process in adults much more than in children.

A basic principle of adult learning is that students should be able to learn at their own pace. This is a common occurrence in many ABE and developmental education programs. Adults typically learn most effectively when they set their own pace and take a break periodically. If an adult is forced to proceed much slower or faster than the preferred pace, learning effectiveness declines.

Educational Implications

To fully use knowledge of the adult's orientation to learning, the following additional suggestions for adult educators are offered:

1. Design the learning activities so that they are problem-centered rather than subject-centered. The developmental tasks approach would encourage this.
2. Be certain that the learning task relates to the personal experiences of the learner.
3. Check to determine that the learning experience is meaningful to the learner. Skillful, but tactful, probing can establish this.
4. Encourage the adult to discuss and react to the learning experiences as they are presented.
5. Involve the adult as much as is desired in every phase of the teaching-learning transaction.
6. Provide the learner with continuous progress reports so that motivation will be sustained.
7. Experiment with various "reward" systems.
8. Remove time restrictions whenever possible. This will reduce stress and allow for self-pacing.

chapter 3 | IMPROVING SELF-CONCEPT

Self-concepts are the perceptions, ideas, and feelings that people have about themselves. They are created through interaction with others and experiences in society. Self-concepts are formed during early childhood years but will change throughout a person's lifetime. The educational experience is one of the strongest forces influencing a person's self-concept. Concerns regarding the self-concept are common with the majority of the adult learners in ABE and developmental education programs.

This chapter is an exploration of the adult self-concept. It is presented in two parts. The first part is a brief definition and discussion of the self-concept as it applies to the adult in ABE and developmental education programs. Characteristics of positive and negative self-images are presented, as well as a discussion of the relationship of self-concept to sex-role stereotyping. This section examines the adult's sense of self and how this relates to the policies, practices, and personnel of many adult learning centers. It also includes specific suggestions for ABE and developmental education teachers who wish to improve the self-concepts of their students.

The second part of the chapter is a collection of seven activities designed to help adult learners and teachers learn about themselves. These activities can be used at the first class meeting of individuals or groups seeking to improve their self-concepts. They are also appropriate as a special unit or class on improving self-concept, or they can be incorporated within regular lessons.

WHAT IS SELF-CONCEPT?

Some adults enjoy talking to a crowd; others quiver at the thought. One person may eagerly attack a new situation; another may avoid anything different. Some individuals will seek out new acquaintances; others are paralyzed at meeting new faces. Some adults try many new tasks and usually succeed; others seldom make the attempt and when they do usually fail. Does the difference between these adults lie in their genetic makeup? Most psychologists believe that it does not. These various attitudes and forms of behavior result from how people see themselves or, in other words, from their self-concept.

Self-concept is not determined by the genetic information inherited from parents. Rather, it is the persons' total appraisal of their appearance, backgrounds and origins, abilities and resources, and attitudes and feelings that culminate as directing forces in behavior (Knox, 1977). This sense of self is a critical aspect of an individual's personality. The function of the self-concept is reflected in goal-setting, planning, and accommodation of contending forces. It influences behavior patterns and adjustment.

An adult's self-concept is built or achieved through accumulated social contacts and activities. The degree of success in life experiences will determine how individuals feel about themselves. It will also determine how positive one's sense of self really is. Obviously, no one escapes some disappointment and failure in life, and functionally illiterate, undereducated, or uneducated adults are particularly vulnerable. To exacerbate the situation for these students, a significant correlation has been found among self-perception, general performance in academic subjects, and achievements in specific subject matter fields (Brookover, Thomas, and Paterson, 1964). Smith (1972) studied a group of students who completed their programs and a group who did not persist. The dropouts appeared less sure of themselves, higher in self-criticism, and more confused in their self-perceptions than those who persisted. They had lower self-esteem and exhibited less tolerance for frustration and stress.

A person's evaluation of self is commonly classified as high/positive or low/negative (Korman, 1966). Adults who are able to deal effectively with failure are those who have essentially high/positive self-images. These individuals possess confidence, dignity, self-respect, and good personality integration. They appreciate their own merits yet acknowledge their faults (Rosenberg, 1965). Conversely, those with low/negative self-concepts lack confidence and have low expectations and general feelings of inadequacy (Rosenberg, 1979).

A sense of self is affected by societal expectations and norms. The way in which people see themselves is based on how society views them in terms of role and status. Since societal views of ABE and developmental education program participants are generally negative, it is not surprising that self-concept for this group is generally low. Two basic areas that reflect the dominance of cultural expectations in the development of self are age and sex.

The self-images of women and men tend to vary greatly. Some have suggested that self-concept, adjustments, and sexual stereotyping may be related. Women generally value assertiveness and competitiveness less than men. Women tend to be more critical of themselves than men. In addition, many women hold themselves in low esteem and underestimate their abilities. This may be due to the frequent dismissal of women's capabilities, potential, and accomplishments as inferior. In the past, a woman's identity and self-concept may have been determined by whom she marries and mothers, rather than her individual worth as an independent person.

The fact that women and men have different senses of self illustrates not only sex differences, but, even more importantly, reflects sex-role stereotypes. Until recently, the role of a woman in our society was quite clear: wife and mother. Women now are exploring alternatives and various combinations of education, work, and family life. These new opportunities can provide for the growth of a more positive self-concept for both women and men. Teachers of adults can help women and men recognize sex-role stereotypes, take them into account, and reduce them.

For the adult educator it is also important to understand that a person's self-concept is not unalterably fixed, but is modified by every life experience. Between adolescence and old age a sense of self can and often does change greatly.

DEVELOPING POSITIVE SELF-CONCEPT

Educational practices can help or hinder the self-image of the adult learner. The quality of the experience may directly influence the self-concept of an individual. For adult learning center personnel concerned with ABE and developmental education classes, it is frequently difficult to strengthen the initial self-concept of the learner, especially if previous experiences with school have been negative. When the adult returns to the classroom, the rewards of learning must be made so great that they outweigh the anticipated fear of failure and pain of learning.

There are numerous examples of adult learners with weak self-concepts and fear of failure. These individuals are afraid of being wrong, of being laughed at, and of teacher and peer disapproval. Adults' perceptions of abilities can severely restrict achievement even though real abilities may be superior to those demonstrated. Low self-concepts are exhibited by students who insist they cannot do a task before they have tried it, offer an apology before they ask a question, and avoid certain activities because they think they cannot do them. They avoid certain situations, fearing failure, thus perpetuating the low-ability, low self-concept perception.

Adult learning centers can do much to make the learning experience more attractive to adults. These centers can affect the self-concept of their students by their policies, practices, and personnel. The direction of this influence will depend upon the center. To enhance a positive adult self-concept, ABE and developmental education programs should establish an environment where the adult feels accepted, respected, and supported. As mentioned in chapter 2, adults tend to resist learning under conditions that are not compatible with their self-concepts as autonomous, self-directing individuals. Adults should be involved in mutual inquiry with teachers. They should be given responsibility for as much of their own learning as is practical, reasonable, and desirable. It must be recognized that the self-concept of a child is totally different than that of an adult. It is imperative to a healthy sense of self that the adult learner not be treated as a child.

Adult learning programs can completely revise their policies and practices, but if their personnel do nothing to foster positive self-concepts among the students, then the efforts of the centers will be to no avail. An adult educator runs a world in microcosm. The teacher's language and behavior affect the emotional climate of the classroom and ultimately the self-images of the students. When teachers of adults doubt their own worthiness and role as an instructor, they are likely to be unable to foster positive self-concepts in their students. When teachers have essentially favorable attitudes about themselves, they are better prepared to build positive self-images in their students. The teacher's sense of self will determine whether the class setting is a warm, open, friendly place or a room that is rife with tension, anxiety, and uneasiness. The words of the teacher can convey acceptance or they can be used to show reproof and criticism. In essence, teachers must know and like themselves before they can help their students.

Teachers' relationships with their students have a great impact on student self-images. Adult educators in ABE and developmental education programs must treat students as adults and be completely honest. Too many teachers fear to be as blunt with their students as the students are with the teachers. Of course, this bluntness must be tempered with compassion, tact, and acceptance in order to avoid feelings of rejection and alienation on the part of students. Adult learners should be accepted for what they are: worthy beings. Development of a positive self-concept is accomplished through action. The teacher's behavior and actions should reinforce trust, respect, honesty, and acceptance by the adults being taught.

The self-concept may be changed by gaining positive experiences. It is important for educators to remember that many ABE and developmental education students are psychological dropouts long before they become physical dropouts. If adults are provided with failure after failure, it can be expected that sooner or later they will come to believe they are failures and behave accordingly. The teacher in an adult education program must present students with success experiences that interrupt the negativism caused by poor self-concepts. The teacher must help them select experiences that provide a challenge and at the same time encourage opportunities for success. There can be no predetermined standards for an entire class. Each adult must be viewed as a unique person with unique problems, concerns, and feelings. It is important also that the teacher avoid making judgments about students based upon their cumulative records, appearance, moral values, or living arrangements. Each learning experience should be a new beginning.

Educational Implications

There are specific teaching practices that help adults increase their positive sense of self. Some are as follows:

1. Encourage the learner. Teachers should demonstrate to their students that there are many things they can do even when the task seems to be quite difficult. If a student does not succeed, this can be used constructively by both the teacher and student to indicate new directions and purposes for future learning.
2. Remind the adult learner that mistakes are part of learning. Both the

teacher and the adult must expect mistakes. They are to be expected, but not to be dwelt upon.

3. Encourage success and foster the notion that success has no substitute. Everyone needs to succeed at something. The teacher should find areas where every student can feel successful. Illiterate adults need to see progress in their acquisition of basic literacy skills.

4. Be pleased with a good attempt. The teacher should offer students aid in reaching their goals, while at the same time instilling a confidence to continue to improve. It is unrealistic to expect perfection or that every goal will be reached. Often, the process is more important than the product itself.

5. Accept students as they are. Teachers must accept their students as they present themselves, with all their talents and faults, strengths and lesser strengths. From this acceptance the educator can help adults to become what they want to be.

6. Emphasize the independence of the learner. The teacher must help students to be themselves and avoid overdependence.

7. Know the students. Know as much about their outside class interests as possible. There are many people and external events that contribute to the development of self. If the teacher is aware of some of these, students can be helped to better understand themselves. Knowledge of the adult learner's interests and experiences can help the teacher greatly in knowing what is important and meaningful to the individual.

8. Use the class to help. It is important that people feel peer acceptance. The teacher should provide classroom opportunities for each student to find this acceptance.

9. Beware of criticism. For the individual with a weak self-concept, even constructive criticism can be damaging. Experienced ABE and developmental education personnel will confirm the importance of the avoidance of criticism.

10. Provide a warm, open classroom with positive reinforcement from teacher and peers. View the classroom as your livingroom.

11. Treat the student as an autonomous, self-directing adult, capable of making decisions regarding what is to be learned. Perhaps all that is needed or wanted is one specific learning mode or a certain learning resource. If that is all that is required, do it!

12. Avoid sex-role, socioeconomic, and cultural stereotyping.

13. Be cautious regarding excessive praise. If the praise is unearned, the

student will know it. Too much praise is easily viewed as evidence of the teacher's "phoniness."

14. Help adult students to make contact with their positive selves. Adults needs to be aware of their values, feelings, beliefs, strengths, weaknesses, and preferences.

ACTIVITIES FOR IMPROVING SELF-CONCEPT

Several activities have been devised to assist adult students in recognizing that they possess many positive qualities and that these should be further developed. This awareness can be used by both ABE and developmental education teachers and learners, to increase personal satisfaction and help foster a positive sense of self. The exercises that follow can be used effectively with a group or with an individual, as they are readily adaptable to a variety of settings. They can be used at the first class meeting to help students feel comfortable and get acquainted or in subsequent class sessions. Some can be used as the basis of a specific class or workshop on the development or improvement of the self-concept. The key is that these exercises are designed to encourage individuals to think about themselves. This process is not limited to one type of class or to a particular subject. It is appropriate for all types of learners.

The activities that follow were drawn from several sources, and they are not arranged in any priority. They should be used and modified by individual teachers and adult learning center personnel. Further, personnel are encouraged to build and maintain their own file of activities. See which ones work best for you in your own context. Each activity will be presented with instructions and a discussion section elaborating upon the purpose of the activity.

Activity 1[1]

INSTRUCTIONS

Read and think about the following definition: *Achievement: a feat, something done successfully, accomplishment, something gotten by effort, attainment, realization.* How does this apply to you?

---

[1]Activities 1, 2, and 3 were taken from "Searching for the Positive Self," developed by the Mesa (Arizona) Public Schools Guidance Department, written by Jan Belknap, Bill Ebert, John Thomas, Alison Vallenari, Keith Vaughan, and Jeanne Woodward. Contact person: Byron E. McKinnon.

DISCUSSION

The things that help to make you who you are include your achievements. But what are achievements? An achievement is something that is done successfully through the expending of effort. How many things have you ever tried to do? Any of these things that you succeeded in doing are achievements. Looking at achievements in this way, vowing to be nice to people and succeeding in doing so, would be an achievement. Some of these you may never have considered as achievements. However, if you work hard to attain something, whether it is within yourself or with others, then you have achieved.

Activity 2

INSTRUCTIONS

List below your achievements in areas that you perhaps never considered before. Fill in at least two achievements in each of the following interpersonal and intrapersonal areas.

Interpersonal—those areas which involve interaction with other people.
Intrapersonal—those areas within yourself.

List each achievement as a specific statement.

I.   Interpersonal
     Example: "I really consider it an achievement when my spouse and I are able to sit down and talk to each other."
     A.   Personal Relationships:
          1. Family

          2. Peers

     3. Teacher

   B.   At the Adult Learning Center:

   C.   Job:

   D.   Other:

II.   Intrapersonal
     Example: "I have achieved being really honest with myself."
     A.   Personal Qualities:

     B.   Interest, Skills, and Talents:

DISCUSSION

It is often difficult to list interpersonal and intrapersonal achievements. This probably is because it is difficult to think about ourselves and our relationships with others. If you have listed achievements in even one or two of the areas, it is a credit to your ability to honestly think about yourself. Discuss these achievements with someone whose opinion you value. This will help you to further clarify why these achievements are significant or important.

Activity 3

INSTRUCTIONS

Select a partner to share this activity with you. You and your partner should respond in turn to each section of the exercise. You may alternate who responds first, but you should both finish each part before proceeding.

I. Focusing on You
    Discuss this with your partner after you have responded to the following points:
    A. Positive personal attributes
        1. Two physical qualities I like in myself
        2. Three personality qualities I like in myself
        3. One talent or skill I like in myself
    B. The development of your positive self-concept through
        1. Two most satisfying achievements
        2. Two most growth-producing relationships (meaningful, happy, pleasurable, etc.)
    C. Present situation—I feel most positive about myself when
        1. I'm doing . . .
        2. I'm with . . .
        3. I'm at . . .
    D. Create a situation (in fantasy) in which you are at your best.

II. Focusing on Your Partner
    A. 1. One physical feature of your partner that you really like.
        2. One personality trait of your partner that you really like.
        3. One talent or skill of your partner that you really like.

    B.   A fantasy about your partner excelling
        1. Where?
        2. Doing what?
    C.   One positive thing that you are feeling toward your partner right now.
    D.   Record your feelings, your thoughts, your memories, and your partner's feedback from these experiences. Keep them for good reading on a bad day.

DISCUSSION

We are frequently taught to look at the negative. Rarely are we taught to stress the positive aspects of our life or our situation. By completing this activity, you are making an attempt to reverse this by looking at not only the positive aspects of your own life but also the positive aspects of your relationship with others. Sharing these thoughts and feelings with a partner helps you to know just how good it feels to share positive feelings with another person.

Activity 4

INSTRUCTIONS

Cut from newspapers and magazines pictures and words that exemplify personal characteristics. Select those pictures, words, or phrases that best describe yourself as you see yourself. Make a collage with the material you have cut out.

DISCUSSION

This will help the students to think about themselves. It is a visual aid in a discussion of self-image. Collages can be shared with the class if each student wishes to do so.

Activity 5

INSTRUCTIONS

You have been given a budget of $3,000. Divide the money according to your preferences among the following fifteen items. Once you have divided all the money, you will bid for each item in a class auction.

Items up for auction:

Items	Amount You Budget for It
1. To have your name as a household word.	_____
2. To rid the world of all disease.	_____
3. To know the meaning of life.	_____
4. To establish your own world based on your philosophy on life.	_____
5. To be the richest person in the world.	_____
6. To be president of the United States.	_____
7. To live the perfect romance.	_____
8. To live to 100 with perfect health.	_____
9. To rid the world of all prejudice.	_____
10. To travel anywhere, anytime, free.	_____
11. To master the profession of your choice.	_____
12. To have a year of nothing but enjoyment—no hurt, no distressing situations or events.	_____
13. To donate a million dollars to your favorite charity.	_____
14. To rid the world of unfairness.	_____
15. To do your own thing without hassles.	_____

DISCUSSION

This activity will reflect the students' values. It can be used to show what they think important, and the types of items they choose will reflect their preferences in life. This knowledge will lead to better understanding of self.

Activity 6[2]

INSTRUCTIONS

Using tag board or other substantial material cut the patterns as shown and mark with the appropriate letters. All measurements must be precise (6″ x 6″) so that pieces will interchange accurately. Place one complete set of five squares in an envelope. (These materials should be pre-

---

[2]Adapted from the JOCUMA material developed in Zeno Johnson, Sue Cummings, and Bets Mannera, Arizona State University.

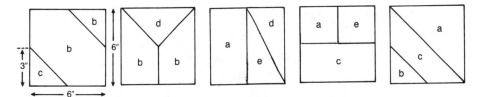

pared by the teacher prior to the activity. One set of five squares is needed for every five players.)

Arrange the players in groups of five around a table or other hard surface. Each group is given an envelope with pieces. Each player takes all of the pieces marked with a single letter of the alphabet.

The goal is for each player to form a 6″ square.

Ground Rules

1. You may pass *one* of your pieces to another at one time.
2. You may *not talk.*
3. You may *not gesture.*
4. You may not touch another person's pieces or take them. You may only accept them when they are passed to you.

DISCUSSION

The key to success is to be aware of what other people need. This activity helps participants become aware of their behavior and the effect of it on others.

Do you look at the people you are with and see their needs? What happens when one person's puzzle is completed and the others' are not? What is being said nonverbally? Could you be saying: "My life is okay— don't bother me. Don't mess up my puzzle."

Activity 7[3]

INSTRUCTIONS

This is a self-esteem evaluation. It is important that you be honest with yourself in order to obtain as valid a score as possible.

---

[3]From "Barksdale Self-Esteem Evaluation #35," *Building Self-Esteem,* published 1972 by the Barksdale Foundation for the Furtherance of Human Understanding, Idyllwild, California, with permission of the copyright holder, Lilburn S. Barksdale.

Score each statement as follows:

$$0 = \text{If not true}$$
$$1 = \text{If somewhat true}$$
$$2 = \text{If largely true}$$
$$3 = \text{If true}$$

Score		*Statement of Present Condition or Action*
————	1.	I usually feel inferior to others.
————	2.	I normally feel warm and happy toward myself.
————	3.	I often feel inadequate to handle new situations.
————	4.	I usually feel warm and friendly toward all I contact.
————	5.	I habitually condemn myself for my mistakes and shortcomings.
————	6.	I am free of shame, blame, guilt, and remorse.
————	7.	I have a driving need to prove my worth and excellence.
————	8.	I have great enjoyment and zest for living.
————	9.	I am much concerned about what others think and say of me.
————	10.	I can let others be "wrong" without attempting to correct them.
————	11.	I have an intense need for recognition and approval.
————	12.	I am usually free of emotional turmoil, conflict, and frustration.
————	13.	Losing normally causes me to feel resentful and "less than."
————	14.	I usually anticipate new endeavors with quiet confidence.
————	15.	I am prone to condemn others and often wish them punished.
————	16.	I normally do my own thinking and make my own decisions.
————	17.	I often defer to others on account of their ability, wealth, or prestige.
————	18.	I willingly take responsibility for the consequences of my actions.
————	19.	I am inclined to exaggerate and lie to maintain a desired image.
————	20.	I am free to give precedence to my own needs and desires.

_____ 21. I tend to belittle my own talents, possessions, and achievements.

_____ 22. I normally speak up for my own opinions and convictions.

_____ 23. I habitually deny, alibi, justify, or rationalize my mistakes and defeats.

_____ 24. I am usually poised and comfortable among strangers.

_____ 25. I am very often critical and belittling of others.

_____ 26. I am free to express love, anger, hostility, resentment, joy, etc.

_____ 27. I feel very vulnerable to others' opinions, comments, and attitude.

_____ 28. I rarely experience jealousy, envy, or suspicion.

_____ 29. I am a "professional people pleaser."

_____ 30. I am not prejudiced toward racial, ethnic, or religious groups.

_____ 31. I am fearful of exposing my "real self."

_____ 32. I am normally friendly, considerate, and generous with others.

_____ 33. I often blame others for my handicaps, problems, and mistakes.

_____ 34. I rarely feel uncomfortable, lonely, and isolated when alone.

_____ 35. I am a compulsive "perfectionist."

_____ 36. I accept compliments and gifts without embarrassment or obligation.

_____ 37. I am often compulsive about eating, smoking, talking or drinking.

_____ 38. I am appreciative of others' achievements and ideas.

_____ 39. I often shun new endeavors because of fear of mistakes or failure.

_____ 40. I make and keep friends without exerting myself.

_____ 41. I am often embarrassed by the actions of my family or friends.

_____ 42. I readily admit my mistakes, shortcomings, and defeats.

_____ 43. I experience a strong need to defend my acts, opinions, and beliefs.

_____ 44. I take disagreement and refusal without feeling "put down," or rejected.

_____ 45. I have an intense need for confirmation and agreement.
_____ 46. I am eagerly open to new ideas and proposals.
_____ 47. I customarily judge my self-worth by personal comparison with others.
_____ 48. I am free to think any thoughts that come into my mind.
_____ 49. I frequently boast about myself, my possessions, and achievements.
_____ 50. I accept my own authority and do as I, myself, see fit.

After you have scored each statement you can obtain your Self-Esteem Index (SEI) by adding the individual scores of all even-numbered statements (i.e., 2, 4, 6, 8 etc.). From this total subtract the sum of the individual scores of all odd-numbered statements (i.e., 1, 3, 5, 7 etc.). This net score is your current SEI. For example: If the sum of all the individual scores of the even-numbered statements is 37 and the sum of all the individual scores of the odd-numbered statements is 62, your SEI is 37 –62, or −25. The possible range of one's SEI is from −75 to +75. Yours will fall somewhere in between.

My SEI (Self Esteem Index) is _____.

DISCUSSION

It is important to not be concerned over the SEI, no matter how low, or even negative. Self-esteem is simply what it is, the automatic product of your heritage and total life experience, and thus nothing to be ashamed or embarrassed about.

The SEI can be used as a reference point for gauging an individual's progress in building self-esteem. It should be stressed that, no matter how low a SEI may be, it can be brought up to any desired value by conscientious effort and an awareness of a positive self.

Part II

TEACHING IN ABE AND DEVELOPMENTAL EDUCATION PROGRAMS

chapter 4 | ASKING AND ANSWERING QUESTIONS

Questions are initiators of response. They are probably used by teachers more than any other technique to involve the learners in the learning process. Since questions are so commonly used, it is logical to assume that the art of asking good questions and responding to them has been mastered by teachers at every level. This is not so!

Very seldom do instructors give thought to asking questions. Yet, questions are a basic tool in the teaching process. Teachers ask questions to motivate, to instruct, and to evaluate as part of the everyday routine in the learning center, yet seldom is much thought given to why the questions are being posed, the elements of good questions, or the types of questions to be asked.

Not only teachers ask questions. In most, if not all, classrooms students also ask questions of the teacher. Frequently, how the question is responded to can make a profound difference regarding the learner's willingness to ask another question or to the continuance in the program! Yet, seldom, if ever, have instructors been taught how to respond to questions.

This chapter focuses on the importance of questions and answers. Techniques for asking and answering questions can be learned, practiced, and improved upon.

WHY ASK QUESTIONS?

In ABE and developmental education programs, the instructor asks questions for a variety of reasons. Perhaps the most obvious reason is to see what the students know about a subject or a topic under review. It might be to see if the adult learners have had difficulty reading or understanding an assignment. Another reason might be to clarify a point under discussion.

Questions may be used as a break from a lecture, in-class reading, or math assignment. More daring teachers might ask questions to get some sense of how effective their own teaching is. A question may be asked simply to encourage the shy or reluctant adult to participate in the discussion.

Questions can be used to get and maintain the interest of the adult learners. Carefully designed, yet spontaneously asked questions at strategic points during a session will not only direct interest but can serve to alert the group to what is coming next. By asking controversial or challenging questions related to the experience of the adult, the instructor can maintain and sustain interest throughout the presentation.

Another reason to ask questions is to direct attention to various parts of the material that the instructor feels need to be emphasized. For example, when discussing fractions, the instructor might know that the class is particularly in need of information regarding numerators. A "mini-lecture" followed by a few well thought-out questions designed to reinforce the points being made would not only provide the needed information but would indicate that this is a special area of concern. Questions that focus on specific elements of the lesson help the students to focus their attention on the more important material.

Questions can stimulate logical or critical thinking. This is especially true if they call for inferences, deductions, or conclusions. These types of questions are most beneficial to learners interested in developing new insights, perspectives, and understandings. Further, they can assist with the ancillary skill of critical analysis.

Within adult learning centers, it is well known that many students are somewhat distrustful of the learning environment. They have experiences and values that may be quite different from those of the instructor. Carefully considered questions by the instructor should draw upon these experiences to supplement and interpret information being presented. This is not only beneficial to the other learners in the group, but serves to build rapport and trust.

Regardless of why they are asked, questions should be well planned and thought out. They should have a definite purpose and should not be used to embarrass, intimidate, or negatively affect the adult's self-concept. As mentioned in chapter 3, many participants in ABE and developmental education programs enter the programs with low/negative self-concepts. An ill-timed question or one that is not carefully considered can damage an already fragile self-concept. When this happens, the result is predictable—the student will drop out!

When asking questions, remember that the same question can simultaneously serve a variety of purposes. For example, the question "What is inflation?" may be asked in an attempt to stimulate recall of the definition. That identical question may also provide a break from the lecture, alert the group to what is coming next, direct attention to a more important part of a lesson, or serve to more closely identify the instructor with the members of the class. Generally, however, the instructor asks the question with a specific purpose in mind, such as to check for comprehension or to clarify a point.

WHAT TYPE OF QUESTIONS SHOULD BE ASKED?

Much has been written about the classification of questions used in various educational settings. One useful publication is Norris M. Sanders's *Classroom Questions: What Kinds?* Based upon B. S. Bloom's *Taxonomy of Educational Objectives,* Sanders presents a taxonomy of questions that facilitates the processing of information at various intellectual levels.

Sanders presents seven hierarchical categories of questions. Each is cumulative in that each type of question has its own unique characteristics, but also contains some elements of all the categories below it. For example, the ABE or developmental education learning facilitator asking an evaluation question would include some type or aspect of memory, translation, application, analysis, and synthesis questions.

Each of the categories of questions is described as follows (Sanders, 1966, p. 3). They will be discussed in more depth on the pages that follow:

1. *Memory:* The student recalls or recognizes information.
2. *Translation:* The student changes information into a different symbolic form or language.

3. *Interpretation:* The student discovers relationships among facts, generalizations, definitions, values, and skills.
4. *Application:* The student solves a lifelike problem that requires the identification of the issue and the selection and use of appropriate generalizations and skills.
5. *Analysis:* The student solves a problem in the light of conscious knowledge of the parts and forms of thinking.
6. *Synthesis:* The student solves a problem that requires original, creative thinking.
7. *Evaluation:* The student makes a judgment of good or bad, right or wrong, according to standards designated.

The categories can be used at any level and in a variety of situations, be it an informal gathering or a traditional classroom, and with all students. They are highly appropriate for use in an ABE or developmental education setting. The difference in the questions asked lies in the complexity of the thinking, rather than the level of thinking.

Mastery of this system of classifying questions can improve the intellectual climate of the basic education classroom and develop critical thinking for both the adult student and teacher. It also assists in writing feedback questions, defining class or course objectives, and leading class discussions.

Memory

Memory questions require the adult student to recall or recognize information. It is the simplest and most widely used type of question. It is not difficult to write this type of question. A major concern regarding it is how to determine the knowledge that is to be remembered or recalled.

It should be stressed that good memory questions will not only assist the learner to recall specific information but will also focus on knowledge that will be the foundation for other higher-order questions. The more factual information the learner possesses, the better the chances will be for success in the other levels of questions.

There are three weaknesses with memory questions. These are:

1. Adults tend to forget names, dates, facts, and figures more quickly than generalizations and principles.

2. Memorized knowledge does not necessarily represent a high level of understanding. For example, a student may memorize a poem but be virtually unable to discuss its meaning.
3. An education concentrating on memory neglects other intellectual processes. An adult student best learns by practice—by doing, not simply by memorizing.

When working on the development of memory questions, it is very helpful to be familiar with the most common key words, which are those terms usually used in the question. By knowing key words, it is easier to recognize, write, and ask questions at the various levels. It should be noted, however, that the level of a question is determined not only by the wording, but also by the level of thought involved. The most common key words in memory questions are:

Most Common	*Others*
where	define
what	describe
when	identify
who	name
list	recall
how	state
	tell
	write
	indicate

Examples of memory questions:

1. What is the meaning of cost of living?
2. What is Columbus Day?
3. In plane geometry, the shortest distance between two points is:
    a. a straight line
    b. a curved line
    c. an elliptical line
    d. dependent upon line conditions
4. How do you spell Mississippi?
5. What is the numerator of: ½, ⅛?
6. Who is the president of the United States?
7. Name the most recent appointee to the Supreme Court.

Translation

Translation questions ask adults to change information into a different symbolic form or language. In other words, translation questions require the paraphrasing of information from one form to another. They ask adult students to begin putting knowledge to work at a somewhat basic level. The response would not show any insight nor would it be very creative, but would be a very basic translation using a parallel form of communication.

Key words or phrases in translation questions are:

Most Common	*Others*
in your own words	illustrate
draw	paraphrase
	make a chart, graph, map, etc.
	summarize
	restate
	translate

Examples of translation questions:

1. Draw a chart of the bus routes from the center of town to your house.
2. Reduce $\frac{5}{25}$ to its lowest terms.
3. Explain in your own words the meaning of the diagram.

Interpretation

Interpretation questions require the respondent to discover or discuss relationships among facts, generalizations, definitions, values, and skills. The adult student must interpret the relationship of two or more ideas. These ideas may be simple or complex.

A key to writing interpretation questions is to assist the adult to discover or use relationships that relate to their experience. The relationships should be relevant and meaningful to the learner.

In addition to relating to the experiential level of the learner, an interpretation question asks the adult to do something explicit. For example, it might call for the identification of the specific pattern or relationship that is clearly evident in the question.

It is difficult to fully define interpretation because there are many related categories, and all higher levels of the taxonomy involve a more complex application of this category. The emphasis here is to work with common sense and to discover the relationship of two or more ideas. These questions do not require a conscious understanding of the formal logic involved.

Interpretation questions have four major characteristics:

1. The questions ask the adult student to discover a relationship among facts, generalizations, definitions, values, and skills.
2. The question is explicit. It tells the student exactly what to do. If a fact, generalization, definition, value, or skill is to be used, it is identified in the question.
3. The question is objective in the sense that usually there is one and never more than a few correct answers.
4. The question may be in either the short-answer or essay format.

Key words or phrases that oftentime indicate an interpretation question are:

Most Common	*Others*
compare/contrast	differentiate
A is to B as . . .	explain
	demonstrate
	defend/refute
	interpret a graph, numerical concept, cause-effect relationship, etc.

Examples of interpretation questions:

1. Which term does not belong in this sequence?
    religion   freedom   power   gold
2. Compare the Articles of Confederation with the United States Constitution.

3. Using your definition of democracy, explain why democracy is right or wrong.
4. Button is to coat as (tree, paint, lock, wood) is to door.
5. Explain the relationship of the Greek and Roman civilizations toward mythology.

Application

Application questions deal with lifelike problems by asking for the identification of the use and the selection and use of appropriate generalizations and skills. This type of question is designed to give adults practice in the transfer of learning. They require students to identify the problem and then to recognize some principle or procedure for solution. However, in some instances they would only have to identify the correct procedure and not actually engage in the solution. Most word problems in mathematics coursework are examples of application questions.

There are three main characteristics of application questions. However, an application question does not necessarily contain all three characteristics as it is difficult to reproduce lifelike problems in the classroom. The characteristics are:

1. The knowledge asked for should enable the learner to apply it to a real problem. (*Note:* It would be beneficial for the instructor to be aware of the various home or work experiences of the learners in the class.)
2. The knowledge sought should relate to an entire idea or skill rather than a specific part or component. For example, the facilitator would present the entire procedure for repairing the brakes on a car and then ask an application question regarding the brakes and how they are used, rather than ask separate questions regarding each of the component parts such as the brake drums, the brake shoes, the master cylinder, and so on.
3. The question should contain a minimum of directions since it is based on previously learned materials and the student should know what to do.

Application questions will be more meaningful if the facilitator has led up to the question by fully explaining the principles and definitions involved. Prior to asking the adult learner to apply certain principles, the teacher should have pointed out why the principles are important. This can be done by illustrative examples appropriately located throughout the presentation.

The application question differs from the interpretation question in the instructional context in which the question is asked. Application questions require the adult student to go beyond simply knowing a theory to being able to demonstrate its use when asked to do so. When presented with a problem in the application question, the adult must independently choose pertinent knowledge and then apply appropriate theory.

Key words or phrases used in application questions (word problems) are:

Most Common	*Others*
consider	apply
how much	develop
indicate	test
	demonstrate
	build
	plan
	choose
	construct
	show your work
	solve
	tell us
	check out

Examples of application questions:

1. Using a map, indicate the possible locations for the cultivation of wheat.
2. If Tom Sawyer can paint a fence alone in three days, how long will it take if three friends do it for him, assuming each friend can work at the same speed as Tom?
3. Consider the map showing the topography of a region, as well as its roadways and population distribution. Assume you are an urban planner. Indicate where you would locate a shopping center, and explain your reasons for choosing the site.
4. Demonstrate how the Bill of Rights affects your life.

Analysis

Analysis questions require solutions to problems in light of conscious knowledge of the parts and processes of reasoning. The distinctions among analysis questions and application and interpretation questions are easily blurred since the latter two cannot be answered without some elementary knowledge of logical reasoning. However, interpretation and application questions require "common-sense reasoning," whereas analysis questions require the student to be conscious of the intellectual process being used and to be able to explain the rules for reaching a valid and true conclusion.

The analysis question is more difficult to use in the classroom than previously discussed types, but ABE and developmental education teachers could use this type of question in discussions requiring induction, deduction, fallacies, semantics, and logic. A primary reason for using this type of question is to prepare the learner to respond to the higher-order questions, such as those in the synthesis and evaluation categories.

Key words in analysis questions frequently appear in interpretation and applications as well. Some key words and phrases are:

Most Common	*Others*
analyze	categories
indicate the	classify
assume	compare
what do you think	discriminate
	support your
	relate
	explain
	distinguish

Examples of analysis questions:

1. From your observation of the videotape, what do you think was the playwright's major theme?
2. "Some people are more equal than others." Describe the process by which the individual who voiced this phrase arrived at this conclusion.
3. How do the data support the hypothesis that women are not treated equally?

4. From our discussion on human behavior, what are two basic assumptions we must accept regarding people?

Synthesis

Synthesis questions require the adult learner to solve a problem in an imaginative or original way. It requires that information previously acquired be integrated into the response. It usually fosters creativity by the learner.

A synthesis question is one that may be responded to in a variety of ways. For example, a synthesis question that would require the writing of a composition or a short story would incorporate the elements of earlier categories but would not have a preconceived idea of the content. It would likely assume a knowledge of the process parts involved in writing a short story while encouraging the learner to be creative or original in content.

This type of question has four major characteristics:

1. There is no one correct answer, but many possible answers.
2. The question allows more freedom in seeking answers than lower categories.
3. In answering the question, the adult student creates a product or communication.
4. The question leads to a response that can be evaluated subjectively by an adult education teacher.

Key words or phrases used in synthesis questions are:

Most Common	*Others*
write	suggest
propose a plan	think of a way
how	formulate a solution
develop	what conclusion
plan	create
	put together
	make up
	synthesize
	derive
	what major hypothesis
	what would be

Examples of synthesis questions:

1.   Write a short story.
2.   Make up a tall tale.
3.   How can we get the community to support the proposed bond election?
4.   Propose a plan to reorganize the welfare system in your state.
5.   How do people view capital punishment in this country?
6.   Create a drawing of what you think the year 2000 will be like.
7.   Propose a plan for a mass transit system.

Evaluation

In order to respond to an evaluation question, the learner must have established an appropriate evaluative criteria relative to the idea, notion, or concept to be evaluated and must be able to determine the degree to which the idea, notion, or concept meets these criteria. Evaluation questions require that adult learners have an understanding of the differences between fact and opinion.

When working with students in an adult learning center, it is important to remember that the values and ideas of the learner may differ from those of the facilitator. In these instances, there may be more than one correct answer regarding a particular point. True evaluation questions will encourage the learner to establish the evaluative criteria based on their values, not those of the facilitator.

Key words and phrases used in evaluation questions are:

Most Common	*Others*
what is	what would you consider
evaluate	choose
defend	decide
	judge
	check the
	indicate
	select
	what is most appropriate

Examples of evaluation questions:

1. What characteristics do you think a superior president should have? Indicate how the last two presidents have been superior or inferior.
2. Which statement below would explain whether the car is a good buy?
3. Indicate in what ways this is a workable solution.
4. According to the stated situation, which is the most appropriate action the person could take?

Summary

Instructors who attempt to classify questions actually used in classrooms may find it difficult to assign a particular question to one category, since the level of thinking required by a given question often depends upon the context in which it is asked and the responses that it elicits. For these reasons, the taxonomy should not be viewed as a rigid classification scheme into which each and every question must be categorized. It is most useful as a guide for instructors to use in planning for a varied intellectual classroom experience and as a rough tool for checking the intellectual level at which most of the questions asked in a given class are directed.

Table 1 summarizes the seven types of questions by providing a definition, several key words or phrases, and examples for each type of function.

Table 1. The Seven Levels of Questions

CATEGORY	DEFINITION	KEY WORDS	EXAMPLE

Memory	The student recalls or recognizes information	Who
		What
		When
		List
			What is the meaning of inflation?
			
			In plane geometry, the shortest distance between two points is:
			  a. a straight line
			  b. a curved line
			  c. an elliptical line
			  d. dependent upon line conditions

(continued on page 64)

Table 1. The Seven Levels of Questions *(continued)*

CATEGORY	DEFINITION	KEY WORDS	EXAMPLE
Translation	The student changes information into a different symbolic form or language	Draw In your own words	Explain in your own words the diagrams's meaning. Draw the floor plan of your house.
Interpretation	The student relates relationships among facts, generalizations, definitions, values, and skills	Compare A is to B as . . .	Compare end rhyme and perfect rhyme. The sum is to addition as (difference, product, quotient, divisor) is to multiplication.
Application	The student solves a lifelike problem that requires the identification of the issue and the selection and use of appropriate generalizations and skills	Word problems Consider	Consider a bus schedule of your city. Which bus should you take to get from your home to the learning center? A woman paid $3.80 for a 50-pound bag of potatoes. How much did the potatoes cost per pound?
Analysis	The student solves a problem in the light of conscious knowledge of the parts and process forms of reasoning	Analyze Assumptions What do you . . .	What was his reason for going to the EEOC? Read the apartment lease. What assumptions, if any, are made in it?
Synthesis	The student solves a problem that requires original, creative thinking	Write Propose a plan Develop	Write a short story. Propose a plan to get the community to be consumer conscious.
Evaluation	The student makes a judgment of good or bad, right or wrong, according to standards designated	Evaluate Defend What is	Evaluate the transportation network in the community and its effectiveness in meeting your needs. Establish a criterion for a fair tax structure. Evaluate the present tax system based on this criterion.

APPLICATION EXERCISE 1:
TYPES OF QUESTIONS TO BE ASKED

Each of the following sentences is an example of one of the seven categories of questions described above. In the blank preceding each example, write one of the following letter symbols to indicate which category the example illustrates:

KEY

M = Memory
T = Translation
I = Interpretation
App = Application
Ana = Analysis
S = Synthesis
E = Evaluation

The correct responses can be found in the key to Application Exercise 1, which follows this.

Topic: Cotton Growing

_____ 1. Fertilizer is to cotton as (clothes, food, house, friend) is to a person.

_____ 2. Evaluate the benefits a cotton crop will provide a small community.

_____ 3. What assumptions about cotton, climate, and soil conditions were suggested in our classroom discussion?

_____ 4. What is cotton?

_____ 5. Propose a plan to get more acreage yield from the average cotton crop.

_____ 6. In your own words, what does the text say about the necessary climate conditions for cotton?

_____ 7. If a field is 60 feet by 80 feet, how much fertilizer is needed to cover it? One gallon of liquid fertilizer covers 20 square feet.

Topic: The Constitution

———— 1. Establish a standard for a good constitution.

———— 2. Compare the United States Constitution to your own state's constitution.

———— 3. Indicate how the Constitution has protected our rights.

———— 4. In what year was the Constitution signed?

———— 5. Analyze the impact of the United States Constitution on the legal status of women.

———— 6. State the purpose of the Constitution in your own words.

———— 7. Write your own constitution.

Topic: The Economic Status of Women in American

———— 1. Compare the economic status of women in blue-collar occupations with men in the same occupations.

———— 2. "Women have been stereotyped in the marketplace, just as they have been stereotyped in their home work" (former Secretary of Commerce Juanita Kreps). What assumptions can be made from this statement about this view of the economic status of women?

———— 3. Evaluate the international plan of action proposed by the IWY Commission to improve the economic status of women.

———— 4. Draw a graph showing the average salary of women and of men.

———— 5. If a man is paid $10,460 and a women is paid $7,380 for the same job, what percent of the man's salary is the woman earning?

———— 6. What is the definition of "sexism"?

———— 7. Write a short story about a working woman.

Answer Key to Application Exercise 1

The following list contains the correct answers and a brief explanation for each item in the exercise. If your answers are different, you should review the appropriate sections of this chapter.[1]

---

[1] For more in-depth information, see Norris M. Sanders, *Classroom Questions: What Kinds?* (New York: Harper and Row, 1966).

Topic: Cotton Growing

__I__   1. Fertilizer is to cotton as (clothes, food, house, friend) is to a person.
Key: Relationship is called for.

__E__   2. Evaluate the benefits a cotton crop will provide a small community.
Key: Student is asked to make a judgment.

__Ana__   3. What assumptions about cotton, climate, and soil conditions were suggested in our classroom discussion?
Key: Conscious knowledge of the relationship among cotton, climate, and soil conditions called for.

__M__   4. What is cotton?
Key: This calls for a definition of cotton.

__S__   5. Propose a plan to get more acreage yield from the average cotton crop.
Key: Original thinking called for.

__T__   6. In your own words, what does the text say about the necessary climate conditions for cotton?
Key: Student is asked to use different words but keep the same information.

__App__   7. If a field is 60 feet by 80 feet, how much fertilizer is needed to cover it? One gallon of liquid fertilizer covers 20 square feet.
Key: Use of specific skills (the formula) called for.

Topic: The Constitution

__E__   1. Establish a standard for a good constitution.
Key: Judgment involving a standard called for.

__I__   2. Compare the United States Constitution to your own state's constitution.
Key: Explicit question calling for an explanation of relationship.

__Ana__   3. Indicate how the Constitution has protected our rights.
Key: Selection and appropriate use of generalizations called for.

__M__   4. In what year was the Constitution signed?
Key: Direct recall required.

__App__   5.   Analyze the impact of the United States Constitution on the legal status of women.
Key: Use of appropriate rules for reaching a verbal conclusion called for.

__T__   6.   State the purpose of the Constitution in your own words.
Key: Paraphrasing called for.

__S__   7.   Write your own constitution.
Key: Creative use of prior knowledge called for.

Topic: The Economic Status of Women in American

__I__   1.   Compare the economic status of women in blue-collar occupations with men in the same occupations.
Key: Discovery of relationship of facts and generalizations called for.

__Ana__   2.   "Women have been stereotyped in the marketplace, just as they have been stereotyped in their home work" (former Secretary of Commerce Juanita Kreps). What assumptions can be made from this statement about this view of the economic status of women?
Key: Awareness and use of intellectual process called for.

__E__   3.   Evaluate the international plan of action proposed by the IWY Commission to improve the economic status of women.
Key: Judgment called for.

__T__   4.   Draw a graph showing the average salary of women and of men.
Key: Different language form called for.

__App__   5.   If a man is paid $10,460 and a woman is paid $7,380 for the same job, what percent of the man's salary is the woman earning?
Key: Word problem calling for use of previously discussed principles.

__M__   6.   What is the definition of "sexism"?
Key: Recall demanded.

__S__   7.   Write a short story about a working woman.
Key: Creative thinking called for.

ANSWERING QUESTIONS

In adult learning centers, learning facilitators are asked a wide variety of questions. They range from the usual content-oriented questions to very personal and confidential ones that are frequently asked during break times, before or after class. Those in ABE and developmental education settings must not only expect but should encourage questions as this is a primary way of learning.

A key to properly responding to questions is to ensure that adult learners feel free to ask them. This is usually accomplished when the learning environment is informal and relaxed, thereby creating a climate that actively encourages questions. As discussed in chapter 2, a fruitful learning environment is encouraged when consideration is given to the physical needs of the learner. The surroundings must be suited to the physical needs of the student: the furniture is comfortable, the heating and lighting are adequate, and the center or classroom itself is decorated in such a way as to be inviting to the learner. The image created is one that would freely encourage the asking of questions.

The instructor's nonverbal messages are important when encouraging questions. Even if the physical environment is inviting, the instructor who glares or scowls whenever a question is asked will destroy the feeling of acceptance while outwardly appearing to be responsive. Finger waving or pointing should also be avoided as this tends to single out the learner and may cause embarrassment. The teacher who stands next to a seated student may find that questions are not being asked because this psychologically creates a situation in which the student may feel intimidated as they "look up" to the teacher. Regardless of the intent, if an adult feels intimidated, it is likely that questions will not be asked. Instructors need to be aware of the image they convey when attempting to encourage learners to ask questions.

In an attempt to elicit questions, the instructor might ask, "Are there any questions?," wait a second or two, and then go on when no questions are asked. As many adults in ABE and developmental education programs have low self-concepts to begin with, they are reluctant to ask questions for fear that they might be laughed at or otherwise ridiculed.

Two suggestions are offered to the instructor who sincerely wants to see if there are any questions. First, be patient. After asking, "Are there any questions?," wait a few more seconds before assuming there are no questions. Adults frequently take a bit longer to develop their thoughts and present them in a form they would consider appropriate. Give them the additional time needed to develop their thoughts to a point where it becomes a question. Second, assist the learner to develop a question by providing specific direction when asking for questions. An example might be to ask, "Are there any questions regarding the relationship of John F. Kennedy as president and Robert F. Kennedy as the attorney general?," rather than simply asking, "Are there any questions about the Kennedys?"

Bergquist and Phillips (1975) suggest that responses will be most useful when they adhere to the following guidelines:

1. Focus on the sharing of ideas and information rather than on giving advice, thereby requiring the student to determine how to use the ideas and information.
2. Focus feedback on exploration of alternatives rather than on answers and solutions.
3. Focus feedback on the amount of information that the person receiving it can use, rather than on the amount that the instructor might like to give.
4. Focus feedback on the value it may have to the learner, not on the value or release it provides to the learning facilitator.

When responding to questions, one should be direct and honest, and respond as fully as the situation dictates. Facilitators in ABE and developmental education programs are particularly encouraged not to launch into a five minute response when one of 30 seconds would be sufficient.

There are times when a question is asked that the teacher does not know the answer. In general, teachers of adults are encouraged to admit this. Successful adult educators should promise to get it by the next meeting, refer to appropriate sources, or otherwise attempt to draw upon their teaching experience in an attempt to provide an honest response.

It is not always necessary to directly respond to a question. An effective instructor will use a variety of indirect ways of responding to a question as this varies classroom interaction and helps to prevent the instructor from being boring or predictable. The Clinic to Improve University

Application Exercise 2 will provide examples of the several ways of responding to questions as well as serving to review this section.

APPLICATION EXERCISE 2:
ANSWERING QUESTIONS

Listed below are five techniques for answering questions. This is followed by ten questions or statements. In the blank preceding each, place the number of the technique that you feel is being illustrated in the question or statement.

1. Redirect
2. Probe
3. Repeat the Question
4. Paraphrase
5. Postpone a Response

The correct responses can be found in the key to Application Exercise 2, which follows this.

_____ 1. In other words, Ms. Romerez is asking if the cell nucleus controls all cell activities.

_____ 2. Albert, what do you feel about that?

_____ 3. Why are you concerned with the way in which Legal Services operates?

_____ 4. Irene has said, "Is a light year the distance that light travels in a year?"

_____ 5. We'll come back to that question in a moment.

_____ 6. Who would like to respond to that?

_____ 7. Have you thought about why you asked that?

_____ 8. That's a good question, but it doesn't relate to what we are discussing.

_____ 9. She said, "Is it King Arthur who was big on knighthood and chivalry?"

_____ 10. She was asking if King Arthur was the king who was closely associated with knighthood and chivalry.

Answer Key to Application Exercise 2

The following list contains the correct answers and a brief explanation for each item in the exercise. If your answers are different, you should review the appropriate sections of this chapter.

<u> 4 </u>   1. In other words, Ms. Romerez is asking if the cell nucleus controls all cell activities.
              Key: Teacher is paraphrasing the question.

<u> 1 </u>   2. Albert, what do you feel about that?
              Key: Teacher is redirecting the question to another student.

<u> 2 </u>   3. Why are you concerned with the way in which Legal Services operates?
              Key: Teacher is attempting to discover a deeper concern or meaning.

<u> 3 </u>   4. Irene has said, "Is a light year the distance that light travels in a year?"
              Key: Teacher is repeating the question exactly as given by the student.

<u> 5 </u>   5. We'll come back to that question in a moment.
              Key: Teacher is indicating that the question will be attended to later.

<u> 1 </u>   6. Who would like to respond to that?
              Key: Teacher is seeking a student to respond to the question.

<u> 2 </u>   7. Have you thought about why you asked that?
              Key: Teacher is searching for underlying meaning of the question.

<u> 5 </u>   8. That's a good question, but it doesn't relate to what we are discussing.
              Key: Teacher is postponing the response as it may not be relevant.

<u> 3 </u>   9. She said, "Is it King Arthur who was big on knighthood and chivalry?"
              Key: Teacher is directly repeating the question.

<u> 4 </u> 10. She was asking if King Arthur was the king who was closely associated with knighthood and chivalry.
              Key: Teacher is using similar words to clarify the intent.

chapter 5 ‖ CREATIVE TESTING

This chapter is designed to assist those who teach basic skills to adults to become more effective and creative in testing their students. It discusses the characteristics of tests and how tests can be used. A number of important factors that should be considered when selecting or designing tests for specific purposes are described. The emphasis is on unusual types of evaluations as alternatives to the standard pencil-and-paper tests. A matrix is included to illustrate the infinite possibilities open to the teacher who is not afraid to use testing creatively.

WHAT IS A TEST?

In general, a test is a technique designed to gather information about a student's knowledge, skills, and attitudes in relation to some subject area. Knowledge refers to memory of facts and concepts; skills include abilities to perform specific activites. Attitudes refer to an individual's cognitive and emotional states. A test for adult students could involve a variety of subject matters, from standard academic coursework, to job-related issues, to life-coping topics like budgeting.

Exercise 1

Indicate whether each of these test items is primarily concerned with knowledge (K), skills (S), or attitudes (A). Compare your answers with the answer key that follows.

_____ 1. Name the eight parts of speech.
_____ 2. Write a complete sentence.

———————   3. List five educational goals in order of their priority for you.

———————   4. In this role-playing session, assume you are interviewing for a job as a cook.

———————   5. List four rules to remember about a job interview.

———————   6. List the five parts of a resume.

———————   7. Write a resume.

———————   8. Define vocabulary words needed during a doctor's examination.

———————   9. Role play a routine health exam.

——————— 10. Solve a percent word problem.

——————— 11. Verbally describe your reactions to a picture of a man talking with his boss.

——————— 12. List the right-of-way laws.

——————— 13. Make a right turn at the next corner.

Answer Key to Exercise 1

__K__   1. The students are asked to remember the names of the eight parts of speech. It is assumed that they will then use this knowledge for the skill of writing good English sentences.

__S__   2. The students must demonstrate their skills in action. It is assumed they have a certain amount of knowledge in order to perform the skill.

__A__   3. They are asked to express their values in terms of goals. (Language skill is demonstrated here also but is not the major purpose of this test.)

__S&A__ 4. Depending on what one is looking for, an observer can gather evidence about skill and/or attitude as the students are watched.

__K__   5. The students' memory for rules, rather than behavior, is judged.

__K__   6. The students' memory for terms is evaluated here.

__S__   7. The students must perform a skilled activity. (Attitude may be revealed here, although the format is not especially set up to do this.)

__K__   8. The students' memory for word meanings is assessed.

S&A   9. The effectiveness of the behavior can be judged in relation
          to the goals of the examination. Attitudinal factors will
          also be revealed in the student's cooperation, patience, and
          assertiveness.

S   10. The students must perform a skilled activity.

A   11. The reaction gives a clue to emotional states and values.
          (Again, language skills are shown here but are not a pri-
          mary focus.)

K   12. The students' memory for laws is assessed here.

S   13. The students must perform a skilled behavior.

TEST CHARACTERISTICS

When teachers choose a test or design their own, there are several decisions
to make about the test characteristics preferred.

Product or Process

The instructor should consider whether the testing technique deals
with product or process. Is the objective to inspect an individual's finished
product or evaluate performance? To illustrate, is it the teacher's purpose
to judge the carpenter's cabinet (product) or to observe the construction of
it (process); to analyze a reader's comprehension test score (product) or
listen to the student read out loud and/or talk about their reading
(process)?

Exercise 2

Indicate whether each of these test items would assess product (Prod)
or process (Proc). Compare your answers with the answer key that follows.

_____   1. A student is asked to write down and explain each step in
             the solution of a math problem.
_____   2. A teacher watches a videotape of students participating in
             a group discussion in order to assess their oral language
             skills.
_____   3. An artist's painting wins first prize in a local contest.

_____ 4. An evaluator watches while a mechanic tunes up a car.
_____ 5. An evaluator inspects a car after the mechanic has tuned it to see if the work was done properly.
_____ 6. A student's written essay is judged by a journalist.

Answer Key to Exercise 2

Proc 1. The students' step-by-step activity is judged.
Proc 2. The students are observed as they perform the skilled behavior.
Prod 3. The judges saw only a finished product. They did not evaluate the artist's painting behavior.
Proc 4. The mechanic is watched while performing the task.
Prod 5. The finished product is inspected. The work done to achieve it is not observed.
Prod 6. Only a finished essay is seen. The judges do not know how the student went about composing it.

Direct or Indirect, Part or Whole

In the previous examples, the products and processes used as tests were directly related to the real-life task about which the teacher wanted information. For example, cabinet making and reading were of interest so the teacher had the students build a cabinet or read. If such a straightforward approach is not possible, indirect measures that may look very little like the real-life task may be utilized. However, in many cases the teacher will know from experience that a person who does well on the test will also succeed in the real-life task. The teacher might give the carpenter a paper-and-pencil test about cabinet making. Answering multiple-choice questions is not like building a cabinet, yet a good cabinet maker might be expected to answer the questions correctly.

A related aspect of testing concerns whether the students are asked to perform the whole task or just a few critical parts of it. In some cases the various elements of the task might be analyzed and tested separately. For example, the carpenter could be given a series of short tasks, such as cutting and grooving wood, hammering, and selecting stains. These tasks need not necessarily be present in the same order or to the same extent as they would be in actually building a cabinet. Nonetheless, these tasks provide the instructor with an indicator regarding how well the student would do on the whole task.

Exercise 3

Indicate whether each of these test items is a direct (D) or indirect (I) measure of a real-life task. Compare your answers with the answer key that follows.

_____ 1. Answer these multiple-choice questions on how to fill out an income tax form.
_____ 2. Fill out this income tax form.
_____ 3. Bake a loaf of bread.
_____ 4. Write out the steps used in baking a loaf of bread.
_____ 5. Write an essay on a given subject.
_____ 6. Answer these questions on the parts of speech to demonstrate your writing skill.

Answer Key to Exercise 3

___I___ 1. The students do not actually perform the task. They only answer questions about it.
___D___ 2. The task is performed.
___D___ 3. Similarly, the actual task is executed.
___I___ 4. The actual task is not performed. A paper-and-pencil test is given.
___D___ 5. The students' writing ability is demonstrated.
___I___ 6. The students do not demonstrate writing skills, but answer questions that are supposed to be related to good writing.

Exercise 4

Indicate whether each of these test items samples a whole (W) task or assesses elements or parts (P) of it. Compare your answers with the answer key that follows.

_____ 1. Students establish and use a budget for a two-month period.
_____ 2. Students are asked to list their needs in order of priority.

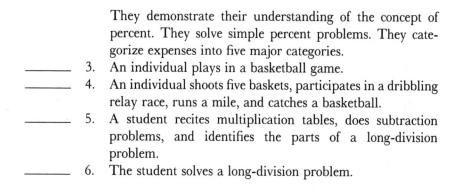

They demonstrate their understanding of the concept of percent. They solve simple percent problems. They categorize expenses into five major categories.

_____ 3. An individual plays in a basketball game.

_____ 4. An individual shoots five baskets, participates in a dribbling relay race, runs a mile, and catches a basketball.

_____ 5. A student recites multiplication tables, does subtraction problems, and identifies the parts of a long-division problem.

_____ 6. The student solves a long-division problem.

Answer Key to Exercise 4

__W__ 1. Budgeting is taken as a whole task.

__P__ 2. Various critical elements of budgeting are tested separately.

__W__ 3. Playing basketball is seen as an integrated task.

__P__ 4. Various critical elements of playing basketball are evaluated separately.

__P__ 5. Skills needed in solving long division are tested separately.

__W__ 6. Long division is taken as an integrated task.

Formality of the Testing

Tests can vary greatly in terms of the formality of their procedures. They can have very detailed instructions that must be strictly followed with all aspects of the testing situation specified, including the exact words of the test administrator, the time limits, scoring techniques, and even seating arrangements. Carefully designed materials can be provided by the test makers. When complete uniformity is desired, little is left to the discretion of the administrator.

For many purposes, however, somewhat less formal tests are adequate, especially when the task is most directly related to a real-life task. If teachers want to assess a student's reading ability, they may simply ask him or her to read a graded passage and note the errors. Here the setting can be quite informal and little needs to be specifically defined by the test maker.

Exercise 5

Indicate whether each of these test items represents a relatively formal (F) or informal (I) method of testing. Compare your answers with the answer key that follows.

_____ 1. A student takes the California Achievement Test.

_____ 2. An instructor listens to a student read, marks down the errors made, and later analyzes the errors.

_____ 3. A student does one or two examples of each math skill needed on the GED test. The teacher notes those that were difficult to complete.

_____ 4. A student takes the math part of the GED test.

_____ 5. The instructor interviews a new student, using a set format of questions and noting the student's answers on a checklist.

_____ 6. Students take the MMPI personality test and their scores are recorded and compared to the test norms.

_____ 7. Students are asked to do several complicated tasks involving mechanical dexterity. The instructor watches and notes their performance.

Answer Key to Exercise 5

___F___ 1. The California Achievement Test requires a procedure that is strictly followed.

___I___ 2. The procedure is fairly straightforward and not rigidly controlled.

___I___ 3. The procedure is straightforward and not rigidly controlled.

___F___ 4. The setting and procedure are rigidly controlled.

___I___ 5. Although there is a format for this interview, it is still conducted with much discretion by the interviewer.

___F___ 6. Here the students take a carefully designed, standardized test.

___I___ 7. This is a straightforward task requiring little formal procedure.

Summary of Test Characteristics

Test characteristics to be considered when designing or choosing tests are:

1. Will the test involve a product or a process?
2. Will the test be directly or indirectly related to the knowledge, skills, and attitudes of interest as educational objectives?
3. Will the test involve the whole task or only some critical elements of it?
4. Will the procedure be relatively formal or informal?

INTERPRETING TEST RESULTS

There is, of course, little value in giving a test unless the results yield useful information. There are several ways to interpret or give meaning to test results.

Norm-referenced Tests

Tests can be designed to tell instructors how their students compare with others. These are termed norm-referenced tests. Such tests must be standardized. This means that the test is administered to a large population sample and analyzed with precise statistical techniques. When this is done, the test developers can report on how the average person from that population will perform on the test. The individual teacher can then compare an individual's score with these average figures. The validity of this procedure, however, depends on how similar the students are to the sample population on which the test was standardized. Other critical variables are how recent the results are and how carefully the instructor followed the procedures indicated in the test manual.

Criterion-referenced Tests

Some tests are not designed to yield this sort of comparative data. Instead of comparing a student's score against other students' scores, individual performance is measured against an absolute standard. Such a test is called a criterion-referenced test. The standards used in interpreting these tests are not established arbitrarily. Much time and effort is extended to arrive at minimum standards for each task. For instance, to determine minimum job competencies, careful on-site studies are made of job efficiency and opinions are gathered from experts in the field. When this is completed, a test can be designed to sample the knowledge, skills, and attitudes that a worker in that job position should have. Criterion-referenced tests are also useful in relation to basic academic skills, such as reading. Experts in the field can agree on a list of minimum competencies that a good reader should have. Tests can be designed to see if an individual meets these standards.

Criterion-referenced tests are a natural outcome of the use of behavioral objectives, because the evidence needed to demonstrate completion of the objective usually is expressed in terms of a behavior to be performed to a specified criterion of excellence. Of course, tests can be both norm-referenced and criterion-referenced if the designers have taken the necessary steps to make them so.

WHAT MAKES A TEST GOOD?

From the discussion presented thus far, it should be apparent that there are a great variety of possible testing strategies—any of which can be effective. In evaluating any test, five factors should be considered:

1. Reliability
2. Validity
3. Practicality
4. Effect on motivation
5. Purpose for testing

Each of these factors will be considered separately.

Reliability

A test must be reliable. This means that the results are consistent enough to be trusted. The test can be replicated by another tester in another setting with similar results. This requires that the test be unambiguous and it must sample enough of the students' behaviors to rule out uncharacteristic mistakes. There are statistical procedures for ensuring reliability that the reader may want to become familiar with (Guilford, 1954; Guthrie, 1981, Lyman, 1971).

Validity

Even if it can be shown that a test is reliably measuring something, there is no assurance that the instrument actually measures what it claims to test—that it is valid. There are several types of validity: face, construct, and concurrent validity.

First, a test may have face validity. This means that it appears to measure what it claims. Although test experts may not emphasize face validity, it may be quite important in ABE and developmental education settings since teachers and students derive the most satisfaction if the test task is clearly like their eventual goal. It will have common-sense value to them.

Construct validity refers to the way in which the test was written. Did the designers have a clear idea of what they were testing and did they carefully base each test item on that idea? Does the test make logical sense?

A test may have concurrent validity if its results are shown to agree with those of other well-accepted tests. For example, if a new, simpler math test is devised, the makers will want to gain support for their test by showing that results are comparable to those of a longer, currently popular math test.

Practicality

Even if a test is both reliable and valid, it still may not be the optimum choice unless it is practical for the particular situation in which it will be used. It should not be too costly in relation to its usefulness and should not involve an inordinate amount of time to complete. Sometimes the most reliable and valid tests may be so long that they will interfere seriously with the activities of the learning center or classroom. They may also be very complicated to administer, requiring special equipment and a carefully controlled setting. In addition, some excellent tests require special training and expertise on the part of the administrator. In choosing such an instrument, consideration of training for the staff members will have to be taken into account.

Effect on Motivation

There is another rather elusive factor to consider in designing or choosing a test. This is the effect the test will have on the students' motivation. Adult students learning basic skills may be especially test-shy. The facilitators may wish to use a less threatening test even if this means sacrificing some measure of reliability or validity.

Purpose for Testing

The weighing of the factors presented depends on the purpose for testing. There are a number of distinct reasons for giving tests, and each requires different test strengths. In general, the reasons for testing can be grouped under four major purposes:

Screening and Placement.   When a student enters a program there may be a need to quickly place him or her in an appropriate class. Screening tests should be brief, nonthreatening, and capable of yielding a rough idea of the students' knowledge, skills, and attitudes.

Diagnosis.   After students have entered the program and feel comfortable, more specific information pertaining to their education needs will have to be ascertained. For such a purpose a diagnostic test would be given. Such a test indicates in detail what the students need to learn. Its results will be used in lesson planning. A diagnostic test usually is longer and more detailed, often requiring individual attention from the administrator and expertise in interpreting its results.

Student Progress.   Tests also are used as teaching tools and measures of student progress. There must be some type of ongoing testing built into the instructional process so that the students get continual feedback about their progress. This becomes a guide for the students and the instructor as they plan daily activities. Immediate feedback also becomes a valuable means of motivating the students and building their self-confidence.

Program Evaluation.   Student testing usually is required as part of a comprehensive program evaluation needed to justify the continued existence of the program. For this purpose, a strongly reliable and valid norm-referenced test often is the best choice.

Matrix

In the remaining section of this chapter, a number of specific testing techniques will be suggested for use with adults learning basic skills. The introduction of these techniques is organized in terms of a framework illustrated in the following sample matrix.

Matrix 1. A Matrix for Categorizing Testing Procedures in Terms of Aspect of Competence Assessed and Purpose for Testing.

	KNOWLEDGE	SKILLS	ATTITUDES
Screening	Trial lesson		
Diagnosis			
Measurement of Student Progress			Classroom Observation
Program Evaluation	Standardized Achievement Test		

The column headings represent the three aspects of competence: knowledge, skills, and attitudes. The row headings include the four purposes for testing: screening, diagnosis, measurement of student progress, and program evaluation. The cells in this matrix can be filled with suggested testing techniques that are particularly appropriate for each combination of purpose and competence. A few of the techniques to be discussed in this chapter have been entered into the matrix as examples. "Trial lesson" was entered in the upper left box, for instance, because this procedure would be a good way to assess knowledge for the purpose of screening or placing people entering a program. "Classroom observation" was entered as an appropriate procedure for assessing student progress in terms of attitudinal changes. "Standardized achievement test" is entered as a useful tool for program evaluation in terms of student knowledge gains.

The matrix can assist the instructor in becoming a more creative tester. It can be used as the basis for a filing system to help instructors keep track of testing procedures they have used or would like to use. It is hoped that the methods to be described in the next section will stimulate the reader's imagination in devising original approaches to testing.

SUGGESTED TESTING STRATEGIES

Screening Tests

Interview Forms. A carefully designed interview form can prove to be a most effective screening device. It may be all that is needed for initial placement of students. Since students often are nervous or apprehensive when they first enroll, it usually is wise to postpone more formal testing. The interview format also provides the opportunity for human interaction on the individual's first visit to the center. The students leave with the memory of the person with whom they talked and the chance they had to discuss their learning goals. This approach is more positive than the common experience of sitting alone filling out unfamiliar forms and struggling with impersonal tests.

An effective interview form can yield important information about the student's knowledge, skills, and attitudes. It should include the following sections:

1. An introduction to the program, presented orally to the student by the interviewer. This gives the student an opportunity to become comfortable with the surroundings. It also reinforces the idea that the center is there to serve.
2. Oral questions and answers that assess verbal language skills.

First, standard registration data such as name and address would be requested in short-answer form. Then, more open-ended questions can be used on such topics as reasons for attending the center and goals for learning. The language used in these questions can become increasingly difficult so that the interviewer can get a sense of the student's understanding and use of oral language. For some students this section would end the testing, since skill needs already would indicate their placement. Others will go on to section 3.

3.   Written questions and answers, the same or slight variations on those used in section 2. Those who have trouble with short-answer questions would go no farther. Others will go on to the longer answers, but their work should be checked frequently by the instructor to make sure they stop before they experience too much frustration.

Trial Lessons.   A new student usually wants to come away from the first visit to the learning center feeling that the first forward step has been taken. Adult students often are impatient to begin and sorely need the satisfaction of accomplishment. If they feel they have learned on their first visit, they will come back again. A trial lesson is one way to allow this immediate learning to take place even before more formal diagnostic tests are used. In addition, it is a form of a screening test in itself, providing an approximation of the students' skill levels. It also demonstrates the students' learning styles and preferences for one or another method of instruction.

The instructor can offer brief trial lessons as examples of the types of activities and materials used in the center. For example, a trial reading lesson could include introducing new words using several methods. The individual's reaction to and facility with each method would be noted. In the math area a simple computation skill could be explained with several different visual aids (e.g., number line, tally marks, or oral counting).

Class Visits.   A variation of the trial lesson would involve the student joining a regular class as a visitor. The interviewer would accompany the student and make notes about participation in the class. Later, the interviewer would ask the student for his or her own reactions and preferences to the experience.

Self-Selection of Materials. Another simple strategy is to have available to the potential students a selection of the materials used in the center, and allow them to browse through and select one or two to sample. Of course, the student should be carefully supervised by the interviewer and not allowed to become frustrated with the work. In most cases, however, adults will pick materials with which they can feel comfortable and be successful. They will choose materials whose format and topics attract them. Consequently, the interviewer will gain an idea of the kinds of materials the students initially prefer.

This approach will give students a chance to become involved immediately with learning activities. It will also give them the idea that there are many approaches to learning and they will have a part in finding the best one for them.

Language Experience. Another excellent activity for the first lesson is a language experience activity. It provides information for screening purposes as well as a learning experience for the new student. To conduct such an activity, the student is asked to recount something personal, such as information about family members, job, or goals. They might give a short autobiography. If the student seems to be uncomfortable with these personal topics, the lesson can be based on reaction to a picture, a newspaper article, or other more neutral topic.

For a student at a beginning level the interviewer would write down the person's words and then read them back. The student then would try to read the passage. A more advanced student could write down a personal passage, read it to the interviewer, and have it read back. In both cases the passage would be a useful screening device, giving the instructor an idea of the student's language skill as well as interests and attitudes. The passage also can be used as the basis for an initial lesson that will be meaningful and satisfying to the student. The instructor can use the student's words for pronunciation, spelling, and dictionary work. The sentences can be discussed in terms of structure. Punctuation and even handwriting skills can be developed from the material in the passage. In addition, the topics discussed in the passage can be used to choose other reading materials or topics for discussion.

While the instructor will want to give diagnostic tests to get a more comprehensive basis for lesson planning, this initial lesson, based on language experience, will be more than just a time-filler. It already will be giving the student the satisfaction of learning and will be a framework for developing a solid student-instructor relationship.

Diagnostic Tests

The following test strategies are particularly useful as detailed diagnostic tools. They will provide the evidence needed to design lessons for the students. The methods discussed in the section on screening tests can be extended to provide more detailed information. For example, the trial lesson format could become very detailed, with many parts designed to judge the student's ability to learn with a very specific technique. However, the following tests are more easily used as diagnostic tools.

Informal Reading Inventories. A popular method for diagnosing reading skills is the informal reading inventory, a procedure that requires students to read words and brief passages while the examiner records their errors and evaluates their responses to comprehension questions. There are some commercially available inventories (Johnson & Kress, 1965; Potter & Quenneth, 1973), but they also can be designed by local instructors. To give an informal reading inventory, lists of graded words and graded passages are needed. Informal reading inventories consist of five parts:

1. A student reads a series of word lists that have been arranged in order of difficulty. The teacher marks down the student's response so that later the type of decoding errors being made may be analyzed. The examiner will record the student's incorrect responses. A comparison of this response with the written word will indicate which letter and letter combination the student has difficulty with as well as tendencies to omit and/or transpose letters. The student keeps reading the lists until a specified number of errors is made.
2. The teacher then chooses a reading passage for the student, based on his or her level of performance in the word lists. As the student reads the passage aloud, the teacher notes the errors made. These errors may include omissions, additions, or mispronunciations of words as well as inappropriate intonation or phrasing.
3. The teacher asks the student questions about what was read and evaluates the answers.

4. Often, the student is given the chance to read another passage silently and answer questions about it.
5. Finally, the student listens to the teacher read a passage and answers questions. This provides an estimate of listening comprehension as compared to reading comprehension.

After the testing is complete, the examiner reviews the notes taken and the types of errors made. This provides an idea of the skills the student needs to practice and an estimate of the reading level at which to choose reading materials for the student.

Locally Made Criterion-referenced Tests. Although there are numerous commercially available criterion-referenced tests, it may be profitable to create one. To construct such a test, these general steps should be followed:

1. The staff of the learning center or the teacher should establish a checklist of the skills to be taught in a given skill area. If possible, the skills should be listed in the order in which they will be taught. Suggestions concerning which skills to include can come from a number of sources, including other instructors and experts in the field, commercially available materials, or commonly used tests. The staff or teacher should investigate the situations in which the students will use the skills they learn: other courses or training programs, work sites, community or home settings. This investigation will help the staff identify the skills that will be most functional for the students. In addition, a tentative list of these skills may be submitted to students for their opinions.
2. When this list finally is established, construct a diagnostic test by devising one or two test items for each skill listed on the checklist.
3. Administer the test to the students. After they complete the test, tally the results and check off the skills they correctly demonstrated. Begin the lesson planning with those skills not checked off.

It usually takes time and experience with tentative lists before a useful skill checklist is achieved. Additionally, it will need to be periodically updated. Such a self-made diagnostic technique usually proves effective because it is so closely allied to the day-to-day curriculum of a specific center. Devising a checklist requires the kind of careful thinking on the part of instructors that leads to effective education. In addition, the checklist provides a ready-made, graphic way to demonstrate to the students their progress as more and more skills are checked off. It is important to remember that the checklist is a tool that should be flexibly utilized.

Self-Evaluation. The value of student participation in diagnosis cannot be overestimated. Students not only gain access to information about themselves, but a productive climate for learning is also established. When student and teacher work as partners in designing and evaluating the student's learning, potential feelings of dependency can be avoided.

Self-evaluation techniques, for the most part, are informal and direct. One method may simply involve presenting the student with a list of skills and discussing personal competence in each area. At the same time, the student can comment on the perceived importance of each skill. This can be done with open-answer questions or with a more specific five-point, Likert-type rating scale. The following is an example of such a scale in the area of consumer economics.

I need to gain skill in filing my income tax.

| Strongly agree | Agree | Undecided | Disagree | Strongly disagree |

Measures of Student Progress

Measures of student progress should be built into programs to provide continuous feedback to the student and lead directly to ongoing planning. As previously discussed, the skill checklist with its coordinated tests offers a straightforward approach to student evaluation. Alternative test items for each skill should be available each time the student is evaluated on that skill. Improvements in attitude can be shown by readministering some projective types of tests, such as writing an autobiography, drawing a self-portrait, or reacting to pictures and situations. In addition, Likert attitude scales and standardized interest tests can be given periodically. Other less formal methods of measuring progress can be used as well. Examples of less formal methods follow.

Teach Another Student. One of the most powerful ways to assess a student's mastery of knowledge is to ask him or her to teach another student. The student must know a subject well in order to introduce it to others. In addition, the need to teach will be a powerful motivation to perfect his or her own understanding.

Oral Presentations. A variation on peer instruction would call for a student or a group of students to present a program to the whole class or even to a group of visitors to the center. While this approach is used a great deal in university education, it is as yet little used in ABE and developmental education settings. There is little reason, however, why it could not be effective for these students, especially in relation to life-coping skills. For example, suppose a group of three or four students becomes interested in how to find and rent a new apartment. They may work closely with one teacher in the center who helps them find materials on this topic, refers them to a representative of the local legal aid agency, and helps them through a series of learning activities. After they have completed their studies, this group of individuals would prepare an evening program open to the learning center community. They would be encouraged to find audiovisual materials, to prepare learning activities for their audience, and generally to make their presentation interesting. Of course, they would be advised to check their presentation with the legal aid representative and to have such an expert present at their program to answer any difficult questions.

Presentations such as this throughout the year can do much to motivate thorough learning on the part of the student groups and to build their self-confidence. In addition, it will also provide an educational service to the community.

Oral Questioning. Very simple, straightforward approaches to evaluation can be undertaken by asking students questions about what they have learned. An informal, oral check can be made easily and quickly to provide a practical, day-to-day approach to measuring pupil progress.

Portfolios. Another way to maintain a continuous record of student progress is to keep a portfolio of their best works. This portfolio can become a source of much pride for the student. In addition, it provides a ready basis for comparisons showing their progress over time. The portfolio can be evaluated by the students themselves, by their instructors, and even by outside experts. For example, if adult learners are interested in preparing for a career in secretarial work, they can begin to compile a folder showing examples of their skill work related to secretarial tasks. This folder can be submitted to an experienced secretary or an instructor in a secretarial school for comment.

Simulations. Much literature is available on simulation techniques for evaluation. Some techniques are quite elaborate while others are very simple, but the principle is the same. A situation is established that duplicates many of the critical features of a real-life task. Then the students are asked to act out roles as if it were a real situation.

In business, for example, there is an evaluation process termed the "in basket" test. The executive-in-training is presented with a desk basket full of memorandums, letters, and other documents typical of those that would face a busy executive on a typical work day. The trainee simulating the role of an executive is expected to deal appropriately with each item and to end the exercise with all documents transferred from the "in" to the "out" basket, indicating that they have been properly handled. The quantity and quality of work in the "out" basket is evaluated by the instructor.

For students interested in job-finding skills, an appropriate simulation test would be a mock interview. For students interested in health-related competencies, a simulated annual checkup might be appropriate. Other useful simulations would include mock accidents, trials, driving tests, apartment hunting, shopping trips, and home repairs. For every job interest there would be simulations related to the specific tasks of the job.

Checklists can be devised so that the instructor could evaluate the skills in the simulation. The simulation also could be evaluated by other students, thus becoming a learning experience for them as well. With the use of videotape, students can evaluate themselves.

All of these simulation tasks offer some evidence in relation to attitudes and values, as well as skills. Other simulations could be devised to deal more directly with measures of attitudes toward interpersonal situations if a feeling of trust has been established within the class and if the instructor is skilled in guiding the role playing. For example, tensions between an employee and supervisor could be simulated. There would be no rationale, of course, for such dramatics unless they were incorporated into a serious curriculum designed to promote greater understanding and maturity in interpersonal relations. Discussions, readings, and other learning activities should be built around the role playing. The role playing can be used as a premeasure and postmeasure of the success of the curriculum.

Case Studies. As an alternative to actual simulations, case studies of real-life situations can be presented orally or in writing for students to interpret and/or complete. This can be done individually or as a group activity. The student responses can be evaluated as evidence of learning in terms of knowledge, skills, and attitudes.

For example, students studying about the driver's manual could read accounts of accidents and use the evidence presented to discuss how the accidents could have been avoided. Those studying civil rights could read and analyze case studies that involve infringements of individual rights.

The case study could be presented somewhat more elaborately if audiovisual aids, such as a slide show or a videotape, could be used to illustrate the case. This could become a group project. Some students could design and present a case study for other students. This project then would be a means of evaluating both the presenters and the audience.

Classroom Observations. As another measure of attitude change, the instructor can periodically observe students as they perform in the classroom. A checklist of things to look for could be worked out by the instructional staff. The form might use a Likert rating scale, and have areas for comments by the instructor.

Journals. Another useful measure of attitude change, as well as improvement in language skills, would be a student journal. The student would be encouraged to write at least once a week with the understanding that no one but the instructor would read it. The instructor would respond in writing to the journal's contents. Although the mechanics of the passage would not be extensively corrected, the instructor could make note of any problems with usage and mechanics, to be used as a basis for later lessons. The journal would provide an ongoing record of improvement in attitudes and language skills.

Real-Life Tasks. Some skill areas lend themselves to real-life tests of competence. For example, a student interested in purchasing a used car could respond by telephone to several ads and obtain appropriate information. Another student could obtain a learner's permit for driving. Several students could plan and prepare a well-balanced meal for the rest of the class. Another example would be to follow a map and determine which bus to take to reach a set destination. Students might do the measuring, figuring, and comparison shopping necessary to buy materials to paint a room in their homes.

Program Evaluation

Many measurement techniques are needed for a thorough program evaluation, and in this chapter, only information derived from student testing is considered. Virtually all of the tests described in this chapter have bearing on the assessment of the program as a whole, but some lend themselves more readily to summary reports.

Standardization tests of achievement and attitudes can provide persuasive evidence of program effectiveness, especially when these reports must be submitted to outside funding agencies. Locally made attitude scales can be developed to yield measures of increased self-confidence and satisfaction or changes in career goals. If skill checklists have been adopted as measures of student progress, then summary reports can include data on the numbers of new skills learned in a given number of sessions.

Other useful data could be gleaned from follow-up studies on former students. Employers or instructors could be asked to evaluate the students' skills. Former students could be asked to comment on the long-term value of their learning, and they might even be willing to be tested to see how much has been retained.

The open house is a valuable approach to program evaluation. This involves inviting the general public to the classroom or learning center, where examples of student work are displayed together with the materials and resources of the center. Short student presentations could be included to demonstrate what they had learned. Such an event builds strong student motivation by providing a great deal of positive feedback and makes all staff and student members feel part of the program. In addition, it enhances community support, helps recruit new students, and even provides some immediate education to the public. Representatives from other learning centers and educational facilities could be invited and their comments and comparisons could be solicited.

SUGGESTIONS FOR FURTHER READING

If you are interested in pursuing the topic of *testing and evaluation* in adult basic education and development education, consult *ABE teaching/learning management system* (1981), *Aspects of educational assessment* (1975), Grotelueschen, Gooter, and Knox (1976), Knowles (1975), Ratteray (1975), Rossman (1977), and Smith (1980). Ideas for *informal testing* can be found in *Adult education program guide* (1975), Griffith (1973), Klevins (1982), and Knowles (1980).

Bibliographies of tests include Buros (1978), Nafriger (1975), Taylor (1974), and Vanderhaar et al. (1975). Johnson and Kress (1965) and Potter and Quenneth (1973) provide simple guidelines for *informal reading inventories*. *Criterion-referenced testing* is discussed in Hambleton and Gorth (1971) and Hernes (1975).

chapter 6 ║ **SIMPLIFYING READING MATERIALS**

Information for the general public is often presented in a written form that is very difficult to read. For ABE and developmental education students, this is especially true. The people who are most in need of assistance in their everyday lives often fail to receive help because they cannot read the literature that describes available services. Service agencies often make no attempt to simplify their publications to match the reading ability of their potential clients. Teachers of functionally illiterate students can attempt to alleviate this problem in several ways: improve reading ability, simplify materials, and campaign for more appropriate written materials from service agencies and publishers.

This chapter begins with a discussion of the readability of written materials. The various factors that help to make a passage more or less difficult to read are identified, and the reader is given the opportunity to practice assessing reading levels using a common readability formula. The remaining sections consider a number of specific steps that can be taken to rewrite materials at a simpler level.

ASSESSING READABILITY

The relative difficulty of a reading passage—its readability—is assessed in many different ways. The most straightforward approach is to present the material to a group of readers and then ask questions about what they have read to assess comprehension. A variant of this approach is the *cloze* procedure. It tests the readers' understanding by asking them to fill in blanks left in the passage. Although there are many simplified ways to measure readability, they are usually verified against one of these two approaches.

The assignment of reading levels to materials is a very controversial topic because there are no measuring tools that include all the factors affecting readability. Those that measure the most factors are time-consuming and difficult to use. The more commonly used methods are more convenient but yield only an approximate level of difficulty.

In addition, the current practice of reporting readability in terms of grade levels is misleading, especially when applied to adult reading materials. The concept of a grade level simply means that the majority of children in that grade in school could read and understand the passage. In other words, a readability level of 7.6 means that the average child in the sixth month of the seventh grade could read the passage. Whether a given passage is easy or difficult for adults depends on their varied experiences, skills, and motivations. Knowing adults' grade level scores on standardized reading tests does not indicate how well they read in real-life reading tasks. Other factors to be considered are the readers' familiarity with the concepts involved, the vocabulary terms used to express those concepts, and the readers' sophistication with language, i.e., the kinds of sentence structures that are most familiar to them.

In addition, an individual's ability to utilize reading materials depends on how he or she will use the information presented. The nature of the written text itself is only one factor affecting the difficulty of a reading task. The level of thinking involved, as discussed in chapter 4, must also be considered. The same written materials can be more or less difficult for readers depending on whether they gain specific facts from their reading or whether they need to analyze and synthesize the information.

Despite these possible limitations, it still is worthwhile to know how to use a common readability formula. There are several formulas that are currently used to assess readability. The Gunning-Fog method (Gunning, 1968) will be discussed here because it is quick and can be used without reference to a graph or table. Once its formula is understood, it can be easily applied. Practicing the use of such a formula is one of the best ways to develop the initial sensitivity for reading difficulty one needs to select and rewrite print materials for students.

Gunning-Fog

The Gunning-Fog method involves the factors of word length and sentence length. It consists of the following steps:[1]

1. Within the text, article, or other written material, select three 100-word samples, one near the beginning (but not the opening paragraph), one near the middle, and one near the end. Do not count titles or headings.
2. Count the number of sentences in each 100-word sample. Determine the average sentence length (ASL) by dividing the number of words by the number of complete sentences.
3. Count the number of words of three or more syllables to get the number of difficult words. Do not count proper nouns, easy compound words like "bookkeeper," or verb forms in which the third syllable is merely the verb ending.
4. Add together the number of polysyllabic words (PW) and the average sentence length, then multiply by four-tenths (0.4), which yields the reading grade level (RGL).
5. Repeat the computation for each sample of 100 words.
6. Compute the average of the three samples.

A summary of the steps, written as a formula, would look like this:

$$ASL + PW \times 0.4 = RGL$$

Example. A passage of 100 words has six sentences and seven long words. What is the reading level?

Step 1. $100/6 = 16.67$
Step 2. $16.67 + 7 = 23.67$
Step 3. $23.67 \times 0.4 = 9.5$ (grade level)

---

[1]Adapted from Gunning (1968), pp. 31–45.

Application Exercise

To further gain experience using the Gunning-Fog method the reader may want to estimate the readability of several sample passages in the following exercise.

PASSAGE 1.[2] A reputable carpet dealer will give you all the time you need to make a selection that will give you years of satisfaction. The Federal Trade Commission works hard to put a stop to deceptive practice in interstate commerce, but sometimes the law takes a long time to become effective.

From the public's point of view there's no substitute for savvy on the part of the customer. So, if you're in the market for new carpeting for your home, and a carpet salesman phones for an appointment, take it easy. If he comes calling with his samples and some handy contracts for you to sign, keep cool. Make your purchase by your own rules, not his.

PASSAGE 2.[3] A cough, the most common symptom of lung cancer, is likely to occur when a growing cancer blocks an airway. You cough as if you were trying to get rid of a foreign object stuck in your lungs. In some cases your saliva is streaked with rusty or even bright red blood.

Another symptom is chest pain. It occurs as a persistent ache that might or might not be related to coughing.

You may develop a wheeze, or hoarseness, or find yourself short of breath. Repeat bouts of pneumonia or bronchitis, too, may be an indication of lung cancer. Like all cancers, lung cancer can cause fatigue, loss of appetite, and weight loss.

PASSAGE 3.[4] When you buy a garment, a fabric, or a fur in a store it often carries a label telling who made it or from what

---

[2]From *Guard against phony ads*. Washington, D.C.: Federal Trade Commission, 1974, p. 3.

[3]From *What you need to know about cancer of the lung*. Washington, D.C.: National Cancer Institute, U.S. Department of Health, Education, and Welfare, Public Health Service. Publication number (NIH) 79-1553, 1979, p. 4.

[4]From *Looking for the label*. Washington, D.C.: Federal Trade Commission, Consumer Bulletin No. 6, 1974, p. 1. (G.P.O. Number 1800–0123).

store it was purchased. Indeed, some labels carry so much prestige that purchasers secretly wish they might be worn more conspicuously. On the other hand, consumers who deal with the cheapest products would be pleased to eliminate labels entirely.

However, there is another label more important than the one showing from which store the article was purchased. When you buy wool, fur, or a textile product from a store, a label should be attached to it telling what the product is made of.

PASSAGE 4.[5]   Lucie Fong worked in a bank downtown. She was in charge of the bank's affairs in other countries. Mostly she dealt with banks in Hong Kong. Her experience in a bank there had helped her get a job in America.

Lucie's job kept her very busy. There was much to be done everyday. She had to make many decisions quickly. And if she made the wrong decision, it could cost the bank a lot of money. Lucie worked under a lot of pressure.

During the noon hour Lucie liked to get away from the bank and relax. Sometimes she went for a walk to a small park to rest under a tree. Sometimes she just walked. She said it made her think better to do something else for awhile.

Answer Key to Application Exercise

PASSAGE 1 READING LEVEL: 13 to nearest grade level. Explanation:
1. 100 words end with "handy" in line 10.
2. There are 4 complete sentences, so $100/4 = 25$.
3. There are 8 polysyllabic words (reputable, selection, satisfaction, deceptive, effective, substitute, customer, appointment),[6] so $25 + 8 = 33$.
4. $33 \times 0.4 = 13.2$ (13 to nearest grade level).

PASSAGE 2 READING LEVEL: 8 to nearest grade level. Explanation:
1. 100 words end with "Like" in line 10.
2. There are 7 complete sentences, so $100/7 = 14$.

---

[5]From L. H. Pierce & E. M. Humbarger, *Reading today's English*. Book 1. Austin, Texas: Steck-Vaughn Company, 1975, p. 118.

[6]"Carpeting" is not counted because it has a simple verb ending "ing".

3. There are 6 polysyllabic words (saliva, persistent, develop, pneumonia, bronchitis, indication),[7] so 14 + 6 = 20.
4. 20 × 0.4 = 8.0 (8 to nearest grade level).

PASSAGE 3 READING LEVEL: 12 to nearest grade level. Explanation:
1. 100 words end with "to" in line 10.
2. There are 4 complete sentences, so 100/4 = 25.
3. There are 6 polysyllabic words (secretly, conspicuously, eliminate, entirely, important, article)[8] so 25 + 6 = 31.
4. 31 × 0.4 = 12.4 (12 to nearest grade level).

PASSAGE 4 READING LEVEL: 5 to nearest grade level. Explanation:
1. 100 words end with "went" in line 10.
2. There are 10 complete sentences, so 100/10 = 10.
3. There are 2 polysyllabic words (experience, decision),[9] so 10 + 2 = 12.
4. 12 × 0.4 = 4.8 (5 to nearest grade level).

Limitations of Gunning-Fog

The Gunning-Fog procedure, like most simplified attempts to measure readability, involves some notion of sentence length and word length. These two characteristics are easy to use and they can give an approximation of the reading difficulty of a passage. However, they can also be misleading. Some short words, for example, can be unfamiliar or can represent ideas that are difficult to grasp. That is why some techniques, such as the Dale-Chall formula, consider more than the length of words and count (instead) the number of words that appear on a list of specific common words (see Dale & Chall, 1948; Klare, 1974–75).

The criteria of sentence length can also be misleading. Some short sentences can be very difficult to understand because the words are arranged in an unusual order or because the words are used in unfamiliar

---

[7]"Another" is not counted because it is a simple compound.
[8]"However" and "another" are not counted because they are simple compounds.
[9]"Everyday" is not counted because it is a simple compound.

ways. Some recent measures of readability try to take these other factors into account by using computerized scorings of various aspects of sentence syntax.

Various approaches to readability consider five interrelated aspects of written language: (1) word length, (2) word familiarity, (3) sentence length, (4) sentence arrangement, and (5) the role a word or phrase plays in a sentence. (See, for example, Montieth, 1976; Harris, 1974; Klare, 1974–75; Seels & Dale, 1971; Williams et al., 1974.)

REWRITING MATERIAL

Since the five factors listed above contribute to the relative readability of written materials, they should be considered when attempting to rewrite materials to be less difficult for students to read. In the remaining sections of this chapter, the reader will have an opportunity to practice using these factors to guide the rewriting of sentences to make them easier to read.

An illustration of the skill to be developed in rewriting materials is given below. Consider the following two samples. The first is an excerpt from a government information bulletin written at a college reading level. The second is a rewritten version of the same excerpt. The reading level has been reduced to a sixth grade level so that it may be used by ABE and developmental education students.

> Every handicapped child is entitled to a free appropriate education, regardless of the nature or severity of handicap. An appropriate education can be afforded by many different methods, including use of regular classes with or without aids, depending on need; in private or public homes or institutions, or through combinations of such methods so long as handicapped and nonhandicapped students are educated together to the maximum extent possible. The result should be to provide the education program best suited to the individual needs of the handicapped people.
>
> It should be emphasized that where a handicapped student is so disruptive that education of other students in the classroom

is impaired, the student can be reassigned. A common sense rule of reason applies in such cases.[10]

All handicapped children have a right to a free education. This education must fit their needs. The children must be educated no matter what their handicap is.

There are several ways to give the children a good education. They can be in regular classes. Sometimes aids can help them there. Some children can be taught in their homes. Other children live in public homes or institutions. They can be taught there. Sometimes, more than one of these ways can be used. If possible, handicapped and non-handicapped children should be taught together. Education should meet the needs of handicapped people.

Sometimes handicapped children can cause problems in the classroom. This can hurt the education of other children. If this happens, the handicapped children should be taught in another way. The school should use common sense.

Rewriting this passage required attention to the five factors discussed previously. Each factor is discussed in detail below.

Word Length and Familiarity

There are many aspects of the written word that cause beginning readers difficulty. They must be able to decode each word, that is, translate it from written letters to the spoken word. Then they must understand the concept the word represents. Shorter words with regular spellings are easier to decode, and more common, concrete words are easier to understand.

Shorter Words. The most straightforward approach to replacing words is to substitute shorter words that will require less sophisticated

---

[10]From *Handicapped persons' rights under federal law.* Washington, D.C.: U.S. Department of Health, Education, and Welfare, Office of Civil Rights, March 1978, p. 5. (G.P.O. Publication Number 1978-258-414).

decoding skills. A thesaurus or dictionary is particularly helpful in this task. In these sources one can usually find a word or short phrase that will fit the sentence. Sometimes minor changes in the sentence will have to be made to ensure it will be correct with the new word. Examples of shorter-word substitutions are:

> The *jubilant* winner got his trophy.
>   Possible substitutes: happy, joyous, joyful
> Repairing the fence was a *laborious* task.
>   Possible substitutes: hard, tiring
> Smoking is *detrimental* to your health.
>   Possible substitutes: harmful, damaging, bad
> The lizard's skin is *impermeable.*
>   Possible substitutes: hard, thick, strong, tough

Common Words.   Words may be more or less difficult because of their meanings, not just because of their pronounceability. In most cases, shorter words will also be more common than long, polysyllabic words but there are exceptions. For example:

> *different* is more common than *diverse*
> *vacation* is more common than *respite*
> *ordinary* is more common than *mundane*

Because there are such exceptions, the shortening rule should not be used unquestionably. The primary goal is to use a word that is familiar to the reader. This may mean using a slightly longer word in some circumstances. Simple compound words are usually commonly understood, even though they may consist of three or more syllables (e.g., housekeeper, serviceman, skyscraper, pickpocket, thickheaded, thunderstorm, safekeeping). Examples of common-word substitutions are:

> His sore foot was a *hindrance* to the runner.
>   Possible substitute: handicap
> The artists were *versed* in their craft.
>   Possible substitute: experienced
> The *felon* was sent to prison.
>   Possible substitutes: criminal, outlaw

Explaining Words. Sometimes there is no desire to change a difficult word. It may be that there is no common synonym for it, or that it is an important or useful word for the students to learn. When a difficult word is included, it should be explained. This can be done by using a phrase in parentheses or separated by a comma. To make it even clearer, it could be explained in a separate sentence.

Sentence Length

Although word choice is important, sentence length also is a major factor affecting the readability of a passage. Passages are easier to understand when each sentence represents only one basic idea, simply expressed. The teacher may want to break down long sentences into simpler sentences. In this section the reader will learn several ways to do this.

Coordinated Elements. The least complicated way to break down a sentence is to separate coordinated elements into separate sentences. Coordinated elements are words or groups of words (phrases or clauses) that fulfill the same role in the sentence.

Clauses:	*It was a bad accident* but *no one was killed.*
Phrases:	There was broken glass *on the sidewalk* and *all over the road.*
Words:	The driver was either *foolish* or *careless.*

Coordinated elements are joined by connecting words, such as *and, but, or, nor, for, yet.* Joining words also include correlative conjunctions: *either . . . or, neither . . . nor, not only . . . but also.* For example:

Not only proper food *but also* regular exercise are necessary for good health.
>Proper food is necessary for good health. Regular exercise is necessary for good health, too.

Either heart disease *or* cancer is the most serious illness today.
>Heart disease may be the most serious illness today. On the other hand, cancer may be the most serious.

Embedded Elements. Sentences are made more difficult to understand when phrases and clauses are added to a simple sentence. These additions give more information about the main idea of the sentence, but sometimes it is advantageous to remove them and express them in a separate sentence. This especially is true when an element has been added into the middle of the sentence. Such extra elements are called embedded elements. They interrupt the natural flow of the sentence and may cause the reader to lose track of the message. In addition, because the embedded element is not emphasized, its own meaning may be missed entirely.

The simplest example of an embedded element is a single adjective added to give information about a noun in the sentence. Usually, this addition does not make the sentence harder to read, but if it is important that the reader notice and remember the adjective, it should be put in a separate sentence.

An *old, used* battery was put in the car.
A battery was put in the car. The battery was old and used.
The dog ate some *poisoned* meat.
The dog ate some meat. It was poisoned.
The *100-degree* heat exhausted them.
The heat exhausted them. It was 100 degrees.

Sometimes a phrase, not just a word, is added to a sentence. If the sentence is to express only one major idea, the phrase should be taken out and written in a separate sentence. This especially is true when the phrase may confuse the main idea of the sentence, or when it needs to be emphasized.

One common type of phrase is the prepositional phrase. Prepositional phrases are descriptive elements, so they are used as adjectives or adverbs in a sentence. They consist of prepositions and their objects. A preposition expresses a relationship—usually one of position (e.g., under, over, on, in, at). Sometimes prepositions may add a condition to an idea, telling how or why.

A salesman *from the Fuller Brush Company* came to the house.
A salesman came to the house. He was from the Fuller Brush Company.

He gave us some information *about a vacuum cleaner.*
He gave us some information. It was about a vacuum cleaner.

Another type of phrase, the appositive, is a noun or pronoun phrase used to explain or identify another noun or pronoun. The appositive may need to be taken out and written in a separate sentence.

George Jones, *an old friend of mine,* came to visit.
George Jones came to visit. He is an old friend of mine.
We knew each other in Franklin, *a small town east of Memphis, Tennessee.*
We knew each other in Franklin. Franklin is a small town east of Memphis, Tennessee.

One more type of embedded phrase is the participle, which is a verb form that acts as an adjective and uses the "ing" ending.

The loudspeaker, *announcing the buses,* was very hard to understand.
The loudspeaker announced the buses. It was hard to understand.
One woman, *looking very worried,* rushed up to the information window.
One woman looked very worried. She rushed up to the information window.

Relative Clauses. Sometimes the embedded element is an entire clause. A relative clause is a descriptive element. Relative clauses begin with a relative pronoun (who, whom, which, that) and include both a subject and predicate. When the clause seems to interfere with the main message of the sentence, or when it is especially important in itself, it should be taken out and expressed in a separate sentence.

Pollution, which *affects everyone's health,* should be controlled as much as possible.
Pollution affects everyone's health. It should be controlled as much as possible.

The person *who lost a brown wallet* can pick it up at the front desk.
　　Someone lost a brown wallet. He can pick it up at the front desk.
At least 281 persons were killed on the American plane, *which was hit broadside by the Dutch plane.*
　　The American plane was hit broadside by the Dutch plane. At least 281 persons were killed on the American plane.

Sentence Arrangement

Sometimes it is not necessary to take an element out of a sentence to make it easier to read. Instead, by simply rearranging the words in a more common order it is easier for the reader to follow.

When he is in traffic, a driver should watch the cars on all sides of him.
　　A driver should watch the cars on all sides of him *when he is in traffic.*
In the puddles, wet leaves are floating.
　　Wet leaves are floating *in the puddles.*
In the trees, the birds welcome back the sun.
　　The birds *in the trees* welcome back the sun.

Voice.　　The natural order for an English sentence is subject/verb/object or complement. This order seems to be the easiest for English speakers to process.
　　For action verbs, the natural sentence order is:

1.　*Actor,* the person or thing that does the action
2.　The *action*
3.　The *object* or person on which the action is performed, and/or the object or person that receives the action

An example of this natural order, called active voice, is:

The clerk (*actor*) gave (*action*) free pens (*object*).

Sometimes, however, the active voice is inverted. The three parts listed above appear in the opposite order:

Free pens (*object*) were given (*action*) by the clerk (*actor*).

Such sentences are said to be in the passive voice because the subject of the sentence is not acting but only receiving action. To make such passive-voice sentences easier to read, they can be rewritten in the active voice.

A home run was hit by the rookie.
The rookie hit a home run.
The pitcher was surprised by the hit.
The hit surprised the pitcher.
The game was saved by that home run.
That home run saved the game.

Roles Words Play

English is a versatile language. Words normally used as one part of speech can be changed slightly so they may function as another part of speech. For example, there are adjectives made from nouns and verbs, such as *joyful* and *usable,* and there are nouns made from adjectives and verbs, such as *fullness* and *construction.* When words are used in this manner, their meaning becomes more abstract. To make them easier to read, the words should be used in their usual roles. Then the passage will be more concrete; that is to say, it will be closer to describing things that can be seen and actions that can be performed. This section will consider one example of words used in different roles: verbs used as nouns.

When other parts of speech are changed to nouns, the process is called nominalization. When verbs become nouns they come to represent quite abstract concepts. For example, *run* is usually used as an action verb in a sentence, but in the following sentence it is a noun, and another word (makes) is the action verb.

Running makes him feel good.

When verbs are used as nouns, they take endings such as the following:

ment	govern*ment*
ance, ence	appear*ance*
tion, sion, ion	disrup*tion,* divi*sion*
ary, ery	bak*ery*
ture, ure	seiz*ure,* mixt*ure*
ior	behav*ior*

The "ing" form of the verb also can be used as a noun. It is then called a gerund. Sentences that have such "verbal nouns" can be changed so that the verb again is used as the main action verb in a sentence.

> *Trying to get a job* took Jane all day.
> Jane tried to get a job all day.

Noun Clauses.   A whole clause can be used as a noun. This is also called nominalization. It represents a higher level of thought because a statement is being made about an abstract idea.

> Today he thought about *what he did yesterday.*

In this sentence, "what he did yesterday" is not just a person, place, or thing. It is a whole idea used as a noun. To make this sentence easier to understand, it can be rephrased. In this case, it is sometimes best to express the idea of the noun clause in a separate sentence first, and then use a pronoun to stand for it in the second sentence.

> Please contribute *whatever you can part with.*
> > You can part with something. Please contribute it.
> It was unfortunate *that the job did not work out.*
> > The job did not work out. That was unfortunate.
> She thought it was significant *that the key was missing.*
> > The key was missing. She thought that was significant.
> *What made him mad* was the rude way people treated him.
> > People treated him in a rude way. This made him mad.

What she wanted to tell you was that she will be late.
　　She will be late. She wanted to tell you that.
What worried him was the money the trip would require.
　　The trip would require some money. This worried him.

REVIEW EXERCISES

As a means of reviewing and consolidating the rewriting skills practiced in the chapter, the reader may now want to try rewriting whole paragraphs.

Directions: Using a separate sheet of paper, rewrite each of the following paragraphs so that the readability level is suitable for the fifth grade or below. When you have completed the rewriting, compare your version with the suggested rewritings that follow. Use the Gunning-Fog process to estimate the readability of your rewritten versions.

PASSAGE 1.[11]　The Office of Civil Rights will take documented cases involving the misuse of financial aid funds. If you feel that you have received an unfair financial aid packet, you can take action which may give you an equal apportionment of the financial aid resources of your school. You must have met certain basic requirements and have filed a complaint within 180 days of the alleged discriminatory practice. We suggest that you file your complaint with the Office of Civil Rights in your region. For your convenience, we have listed the names of the Regional Offices and their addresses below. [A list of offices follows this paragraph.]

PASSAGE 2.　Jose, a man from Mexico who didn't speak English well, came to work at our shop. He was given the oldest tools, the ones Bob used to use. Jose, feeling a little unsure of himself, didn't complain, but he was not happy in the shop. Lonely and discouraged, he didn't talk to anyone and sat by himself in the lunchroom during break times. Jose, not understanding shop procedures, made many mistakes that made Mr. Smith, the shop owner, angry.

---

[11]From OCR Field Offices, *United Scholarship News,* II, No. 5 (April 1975), p. 3.

Then Don, also from Mexico, helped Jose out by explaining the rules in Spanish. Jose, who gained in confidence every day, was soon one of the best workers.

PASSAGE 3.[12]   You have made inquiry about the Public Assistance programs. If you have expressed a desire to make application for any type of assistance, a copy of this booklet and an application have been sent to you. After reading this booklet carefully, complete the application for the type of assistance you desire and sign it. In most instances an individual can qualify for only one type of assistance. If you need help understanding the assistance programs or completing your application, you may obtain it by contacting your County Welfare Office. An application issued must be completed, signed, and returned to the County Welfare Office within 10 days or it will be assumed you do not wish to make application for assistance.

PASSAGE 4.   John endeavors to see his physician periodically for an examination. He just wants to be sure that nothing is wrong. John is disheartened by the fact of his obesity. He has requested a restrictive diet from the doctor but has never been able to persevere with it. He always finds a way to make exceptions to his diet and disobey the doctor's instructions. He knows his behavior is reprehensible, but he cannot regulate his compulsion for food.

He realizes that he should try to get more exercise but the exertion of running always debilitates him for days. He has considered associating with an organization for overweight individuals, but always procrastinates.

Suggested Rewritings

The following are rewritten versions of passages 1–4. Your version need not conform to these samples as there are many equally good ways to rewrite passages. Use your own judgment to evaluate your work but do check to see if you have used a variety or combinations of the techniques presented in this chapter.

---

[12]From *Public assistance in Arizona.* Arizona State Department of Public Welfare, pamphlet 001, November 1972, p. i.

REWRITTEN PASSAGE 1.   Some people do not give out financial aid fairly. Maybe you can prove that this has happened to you. If so, the Office of Civil Rights will listen to you. Someone may have given you an unfair financial aid packet. You can do something about that. There is aid money at your school. You can get a fair share. To do this, you must do certain things. You must also complain to the nearest Office of Civil Rights. Do not wait more than 180 days to do this. The 180 days start on the day they give you a financial aid packet. Here is a list of the Offices of Civil Rights. Find the one closest to you. Complain to that office. [The list of offices follows this paragraph.]

REWRITTEN PASSAGE 2.   Jose came to work at our shop. He is from Mexico. He didn't speak English well. He was given some tools. They were old. Bob used to use those tools. Jose felt a little unsure of himself. He didn't complain.

But Jose was not happy in the shop. He felt lonely and discouraged. He didn't talk to anyone. He sat by himself in the lunchroom during break times. Jose didn't understand how things were done in the shop. He made many mistakes. Mr. Smith was mad about that. Mr. Smith is the boss at the shop.

Don is also from Mexico. He helped Jose. He explained the rules in Spanish. Jose gained confidence every day. Soon he was one of the best workers.

REWRITTEN PASSAGE 3.   You have asked about the Public Assistance programs. If you told us that you wanted to apply for some help from Public Assistance, a copy of this booklet and an application have been sent to you. After reading this booklet carefully, complete the application for the type of help you want and sign it. In most cases, an individual can get only one type of help. If you need help understanding the Public Assistance program or completing your application, you may get it by asking the County Welfare Office. When an application is given to you, you must sign it and return it to the County Welfare Office within 10 days or we will decide you do not wish to apply for help.

REWRITTEN PASSAGE 4.   John tries to see his doctor every so often for a checkup. He just wants to be sure that nothing is wrong. John is worried by the fact that he is overweight. He has asked for a strict diet from the doctor but has never been able to stick to it. He always finds a way to go off his diet and not obey his doctor's advice. He knows his actions are wrong, but he cannot control his need for food.

He knows that he should try to get more exercise, but the effort of running always wears him out for days. He has thought of joining a club for overweight people, but he always puts it off.

CONCLUSION

When rewriting sentences, there is sometimes a concern that interesting sentences are being changed to dull and monotonous forms. This may well be true in some instances, but for the unsophisticated reader the dullness is offset by the pleasure of independently grasping the meaning of what is read. Clarity at times is more important than variety, especially when the information is very important.

As part of a concern for ABE and developmental education students, instructors should campaign for simpler writing in the materials that are directed to them. This would include government and public service pamphlets, as well as advertisements and standardized forms.

However, all the emphasis cannot be placed on providing simplified reading materials. Instructors also need to work with their students to help them understand more complex writing. One effective way to do this is to show students how to do the exercises in this chapter *in reverse*. They could learn to combine sentences using embedded elements, for instance, or to rearrange sentences so as to produce more unusual word orders. They could practice using a thesaurus or dictionary to replace simple words with less common synonyms.

The materials and skills presented in this chapter are helpful in many ways in planning meaningful activities for adult students: They will help the teacher to choose reading materials more easily; to rewrite materials into simpler, more readable forms; and to help students improve their reading skills.

SUGGESTIONS FOR FURTHER READING

For further information about the measurement of *readability* consult Harris (1974), Klare (1974–75), Montieth (1976), Seels and Dale (1971) and Williams (1974). To learn more about *selecting* appropriate reading materials see Berg and Wallace (1980), Beris (1982), Checklist for evaluating adult basic education reading materials (1981), Easy adult reading materials (1973), O'Brien (1980), and Sherman and Buchanan (1980). To further your skill in *rewriting* materials see Gunning (1968), Klare and Buck (1954), Leonard (1980), and Walmsley (1981).

chapter 7 | BASIC READING METHODS

This chapter is designed to assist ABE and developmental education personnel in gaining familiarity with four basic approaches for teaching beginning reading. Each approach's rationale, as well as the typical instructional techniques and materials that it uses, is discussed. The chapter will give the instructor an opportunity to gain empathy for the beginning reader because he or she will be asked to participate as a student, learning to read with an unfamiliar code alphabet.

The four approaches of teaching reading presented are:

1. The phonic approach, learning to associate sounds with individual letters
2. The sight approach, learning to recognize whole words
3. The word-pattern approach, learning to utilize spelling patterns to recognize words and syllables
4. The language-experience approach, learning to read words in the context of one's own language

There are other methods and numerous variations on these methods, but these four have historically been the most frequently used and discussed by educators. They illustrate the wide variety of possible approaches. Each method will be described in its pure or most extreme form in order to make the distinctions among the methods clear. Any actual program would normally represent a modification and/or combination of methods.

It is only fair to preface this chapter by admitting that adult educators do not yet know what is the best way to teach beginning reading. After years of research, discussion, and practical experience, opinions are still divided and there is no conclusive evidence to support one method over another. This is especially true with regard to adult literacy programs, about which little formal research exists.

Advocates of a particular method usually try to justify their choice, and the arguments can sound convincing. However, these justifications often deal with information about the structure of language itself or about the behavior of experienced readers. While these two topics are interesting, neither really explains how to help new adult readers. Simply because a certain method has proven effective for language scholars is no assurance that it will be useful to people just learning to read. Also, information about how people read after years of experience may have very little to say about what they were doing when they were first learning. When research does attempt to compare the effectiveness of one method of teaching reading over another, there are usually so many important factors left uncontrolled that the results cannot be conclusive. What is needed, but not yet available, is a body of careful research dealing directly with adult students and how they first learn to read.

Perhaps the most that can be said at the present time is that there are methods that seem to work for particular teachers with particular students and that many of the most successful instructors use a combination of several methods. They design tailor-made lessons to fit the strengths and preferences of both their students and themselves.

In this chapter, the reader will be introduced to four basic approaches to the teaching of beginning reading. After each approach is described, the reader will be given the opportunity to experience what it is like for a beginning adult reader using this approach. A script for a simulated lesson will be provided so that the reader can play the role of student. In this lesson, an artificial code will be used in place of the English alphabet. Obviously, these simulated lessons are meant for the readers of this book, not for beginning reading students. However, the formats used in the lessons can provide a model for instructors who want to design similar lessons, in the English alphabet, for their students. In addition, the sample worksheets, included as part of these simulated lessons, are typical of the type of written exercises teachers could prepare in the English alphabet when using each method.

The following glossary defines the terms used when discussing the basic methods of teaching reading.

GLOSSARY OF TERMS

AUDITORY. Relating to or experienced through hearing.

BLENDING. Combining phonemes smoothly to make an integrated syllable.

CONSONANT. Any speech sound that is not a vowel (see vowel).

DECODING. The process of analyzing (or pronouncing) a written word on the basis of knowledge about phonemes and word structure.

GRAPHEME. An alphabetic symbol (a letter or letter combination) used to represent a speech sound.

LINGUIST. One who studies languages.

LINGUISTICS. The formal study of languages.

PHONEME. A single speech sound; the smallest unit of sound in a language that can be distinguished by a native speaker.

REVERSAL. A reading error caused by reading a letter as its mirror image or a word as if its letters were written in the reverse order.

SYLLABLE. A unit of spoken language next biggest after a phoneme, consisting of a vowel sound alone or with one or more consonant sounds.

TRANSPOSITION. A reading error caused by reading a string of letters as if they were written in a different order.

VOWEL. A speech sound made without blocking the breath canal. In English, the vowels are the various sounds associated with the letters *a, e, i, o, u,* and *y.*

THE PHONICS METHOD

Rationale

The phonics approach is based on the fact that written English uses an alphabetic system of notation. The individual symbols do not stand for whole words or even entire syllables but rather for individual sounds called phonemes. The phonemes are the smallest pronounceable units in the language. In English, letters or combinations of letters represent phonemes. For example, the letter *s* in English stands for the sound /sss/, as in *sun.*

The strictest phonics method will be discussed here. It is called synthetic phonics. Two skills are the bases of the synthetic method: (1) giving the correct sound (phoneme) for a given letter (grapheme), and (2) blending phonemes into syllables. Proponents of this phonics method want to teach new readers the individual letter sounds in isolation first. The students learn to say /sss/ every time they are shown the letter symbol *s*. Then they learn to blend the letter sounds together to form syllables and words. For example, when shown the syllable *at,* the students would learn to sound out each phoneme one at a time—/a/ and /t/—and then "blend" or put them together to say the word /at/.

The defenders of the phonics method feel that students become independent readers much more quickly because they are given the tools they need to read words they have never seen before. They can decode words without the teacher's help. The phonics advocates cite research showing that English spelling is not as irregular as some people believe. Of course, there is not a simple one-to-one relationship between each phoneme and grapheme. One phoneme might be represented by several graphemes in the way that the sound /s/ is represented by both the letter *s* and the letter *c*. One letter can represent more than one sound, as the letter *c* represents both the sound /s/ and the sound /k/. Nonetheless, the relationship between phonemes and graphemes is not haphazard. It is very much rule-governed. When the readers gain experience with written English, they are able to anticipate what sound any letter will have in a given word. In fact, most experts say that approximately 85 percent of written English is regular or rule-governed. This leaves only a small number of words that must actually be memorized. The rest can be "sounded out" or decoded from written form into spoken form by the reader.

Opponents of phonics instruction point out that the frustrating thing about written English is that this small number of irregular words happens to include frequently used words, such as most of the function words (prepositions, articles, and conjunctions) and many of the most common verbs. Therefore, even the strictest phonics programs must introduce some of these irregular words as sight words right away in order to make meaningful reading passages. However, this does not change the fact that the primary emphasis is on the decoding or sounding-out skill.

Treatment of Auditory Skills

Emphasis is placed on the development of auditory skills in a phonics program. Since nonreaders are not accustomed to dealing with phonemes in isolation, they must spend time learning to (1) discriminate one phoneme from another, (2) produce the phonemes themselves, and (3) blend phonemes together into syllables. These skills can first be practiced orally without the use of written symbols. A second stage would then involve matching the sounds to the written letters.

It should be noted that these auditory skills may be particularly difficult for adult students because of the loss of auditory acuity that begins in the late teens. This has been discussed in chapter 2. Students may need additional cues from lipreading or feeling their own muscle movements as they form the sounds. Identifying letter sounds by hearing alone may not be possible, especially for very similar sounds such as /t/ and /d/, /b/ and /p/, or /k/ and /g/. These letter-recognition skills are important for the new reader, but special help may be needed.

The following are typical exercises an instructor can use to develop auditory skills:

Listen to sounds I make. Are they the same or different? /s/ /m/.
Raise your hand whenever you hear me make the sound /s/.
  /m/ /s/ /v/ /s/ /b/ /s/.
Repeat after me: /s/. [/s/]   /m/. [/m/]
I'll say three sounds slowly. You tell me what they would say if they
  were blended together: /m/ /a/ /n/. [man]

Treatment of Visual Skills

New readers, no matter what method they are using, must also spend much time becoming familiar with individual graphemes (letters) because they will not yet be sensitive to what distinguishes one letter or one letter pattern from another. Their eyes must become attuned to details such as the difference between *o* and *c,* or *h* and *n,* or *n* and *r.* Perhaps the most troublesome new distinction for the new reader is that of orientation. This quality refers to the direction the letter is facing and would include the differences between *p, q,* and *g,* and the differences between *b* and *d.*

This difficulty is particularly hard to overcome because most learning in everyday life runs counter to it. One of the most powerful principles learned through observing the world is that of object permanence. This principle prescribes that an object is still the same object even if it is turned around or put in a new position. In other words, orientation does not make a difference. If a chair is turned around, it is still the same chair. If the letter *b* is turned around, however, it is not a *b* anymore; it has changed its identity and is now a *d*.

The instructor for each of the methods to be discussed in this chapter must deal with this difficult learning task. It is believed that simply through increasing exposure to letters the problem will correct itself, except for those few students with a learning disability. This letter confusion is something to be expected, and the main objective should be to keep students from becoming frustrated by it. To aid the students, however, instructors will very often use exercises like the following:

Circle the letters that are like the first letter:

b/ d b d b b d d b d d b d

Trace the following letter. Then write it three more times on the line. Say the sound of the letter as you write it.

b ————————————————

Another visual skill to be developed involves the proper sequencing of letters within words. One instance of this need comes with reversible words, such as *was* and *saw, on* and *no*. Again, most learning in everyday experience has taught that this reversal of order does not make a difference in the identity of things. A train is still the same train if seen from the other side of the track, but the word *no* if seen from the other side is not the same word.

In most visual tasks, the order of items in a series is not crucial. Objects in a group can be rearranged in many ways and still remain the same group—a basket of fruit, a tool box, a suitcase—but the words *slat* and *salt* are not at all the same. The strict adherence to a left-right sequence is a new coordination skill that must be practiced.

The phonics proponent believes that the blending drills used in the phonics method help to avoid this difficulty since they instill the automatic habit of examining one letter at a time from left to right and combining them according to this left-right sequence. Students are often told to follow the teacher's finger or to use their own fingers to point to each letter as a guide for their visual scanning.

Other visual coordination tasks of importance are the general ability to focus on small print, to scan a line of print from left to right without mistakenly jumping up or down a line, and segmenting words and sentences correctly. It is easy to see that there are many visual skills that cannot be taken for granted by the teacher of new readers. Reading can be an exceedingly difficult task, especially for adults who have spent a lifetime becoming proficient in other sorts of visual tasks. These proficiencies often work against the new skills or habits students must use in reading. The new readers will easily become tired and discouraged.

Treatment of Meaning

Since the primary objective of a beginning lesson in a phonics program is to develop decoding skills, words are not chosen primarily because of their meaningfulness to the student but rather because they use the letter sounds that the program is currently teaching. Usually, the first lessons will use two- and three-letter words formed from one vowel and several consonant letters. Gradually, more letters are introduced and a larger set of possible words is derived from them.

Letter combinations used in drills do not have to be real words. Nonsense syllables are included because they represent possible combinations of the letters the beginning reader knows. Phonics teachers often justify this by saying that longer words are made up of individual syllables that by themselves are nonsense. A student who has only decoded real words will be confused when trying to sound out the syllables of long words. For the teacher of adults, this inclusion of nonsense syllables allows immediate use of longer words with the student, especially if the words are segmented into syllables. For instance, a student who only knows the vowels *a* and *i* and a few consonants can read such words as *fantastic, tactic,* and *impractical,* if they are written in syllables: fan tas tic; tac tic; im prac tic al.

Early stories based on the decoding of words are often stilted, even when a few sight words are introduced, since the bulk of the words come from a very limited pool. For example, an early story might be limited to words made from *s, m, a, t,* and *n,* with the sight words *on, is,* and *the:*

Sam sat on a mat.   The mat is tan.
Nan sat on the mat.   Sam and Nan sat on a tan mat.
Is the mat tan?

The strictest phonics methods would not rely on pictures at all, nor would they introduce the lesson by getting students to relate their own experiences on the subject of the story. The whole idea of the reading exercise is to get the students to practice their decoding skills. Nothing else should interfere. If students guess words by looking at a picture they have not strengthened their ability to read unfamiliar words. However, after the story has been read, the instructors can introduce pictures, discussions, and other activities so the students will "read for meaning."

Sample Lesson

This lesson is typical in design and content of the phonic method, but it uses a code alphabet that will be unfamiliar to the reader (see Chart 1, Alphabet Code Chart). In this lesson the participant will gain an understanding of what it is like to be a beginning reader. Of course, the tasks are considerably easier for one who has already developed reading skills

Chart 1: Alphabet Code Chart

A	______	□	N	______	∩
B	______	≬	O	______	Γ
C	______	∞	P	______	⊼
D	______	↻	Q	______	⋕
E	______	∮	R	______	∵
F	______	↔	S	______	△
G	______	≅	T	______	≪
H	______	∅	U	______	≠
I	______	≈	V	______	∈
J	______	∫	W	______	∥
K	______	⇋	X	______	⊥
L	______	∝	Y	______	⋚
M	______	⊙	Z	______	≡

with a regular alphabet and who only needs to transfer those skills to a new alphabet. Nonreaders will experience the difficulty of becoming familiar with a strange code but will also need to gain many new auditory and visual skills as well as new attitudes. They will not have the self-image of themselves as readers nor the confidence built through successful reading experience. An adult nonreader approaching the world of literacy for the first time experiences many frustrations.

For this and other sample lessons in this chapter, choose a partner and take turns acting as teacher and student. Directions for the teacher will be marked "T," and the student responses will be marked "S."

STEP 1

T: (Points to the symbol.) Look at this letter. It says /m/. What does it say?

S: /m/.

T: That's right, /m/. Whenever I point to this letter, you say /m/.

STEP 2

T: (Points to the symbol.) It says /a/, as in *at*. What does it say?

S: /a/.

T: That's right, /a/. Whenever I point to this letter, you say /a/.

STEP 3

T: Now we are going to learn to blend. Watch me blend first. (Point to the □ and make the sound /a/. Keep making the sound /a/ as you begin to move your finger along the arrow. As soon as your finger is below the ⊙, begin to make the /m/ sound.)

T: Blend it. /am/. This is the word *am*. I read the word *am*.

STEP 4

T: Now you try. When I point to the letter, you make
   its sound and keep on making it until I point to the
   next letter. (Point to the □.)
S: /a/.
T: (Move your finger along the arrow until it is under
   the ⊙.)
S: /m/.
T: Blend it.
S: /am/.
T: What word is this?
S: *am.*
T: You read the word *am.*

STEP 5

T: (Points to the symbol.) Look at this letter; it says
   /s/. What does it say?
S: /s/.
T: That's right, /s/.

STEP 6

T: (Points to the symbol.) This says /n/. What does
   it say?
S: /n/.
T: That's right, /n/.

STEP 7

T: (Points to the symbol.) This says /i/, as in *it.*
   What does it say?
S: /i/.
T: That's right, /i/.

STEP 8

T:　(Points to the symbol.) This says /t/. What does
　　it say?

S:　/t/.

T:　That's right, /t/.

STEP 9

T:　Follow my finger to say the sounds in each of these
　　words. (Point to each sound in order as the student
　　makes the sounds. In our regular alphabet, the
　　words are: Sam, man, in, sin, sit, sits.)

T:　Blend it. (Student should blend the sounds into the
　　correct word. *Note:* If the student forgets the sound
　　of one of the symbols, restate the sound and start
　　the word over again.)

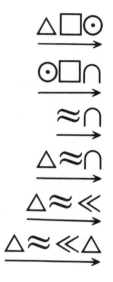

STEP 10

T:　Look at this word. It says /the/. What does it say?

S:　/the/.

T:　That's right, /the/.

STEP 11

T:　Look at this word. It says /on/. What does it say?

S:　/on/.

T:　That's right, /on/.

STEP 12

T: Now we will read a short story. (Repeat the blending drill of Step 9
    for each word in the story in figure 11. After each period, have the
    student read back the entire sentence without blending. After all the
    sentences have been read this way, read the entire passage with the
    student. Then have the student read it alone. In our regular alphabet,
    the story reads: A man sits on a mat. It is a tan mat. The man is Sam.
    Sam is tan. Sam sits. Sam is tan.)

□ ⊙□∩ △≈≪△ ⌐∩ □ ⊙□≪.

≈≪ ≈△ □ ≪□∩ ⊙□≪.

≪∅ʃ ⊙□∩ ≈△ △□⊙.

△□⊙ ≈△ ≪□∩.

△□⊙ △≈≪△.

△□⊙ ≈△ ≪□∩.

Sample Worksheet

The teacher gives the student a phonics worksheet and reads the following instructions.

PART 1

T: Point to the letter whose sound I say. /s/, /n/, /a/, /i/, /t/, and /m/.

PART 2

T: Write the letter for each sound I say. /i/, /s/, /a/, /t/, /m/, and /n/.

PART 3

T: Fill in the missing letters to match the pictures.

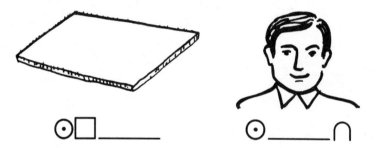

PART 4

T: Match the words to the correct picture.

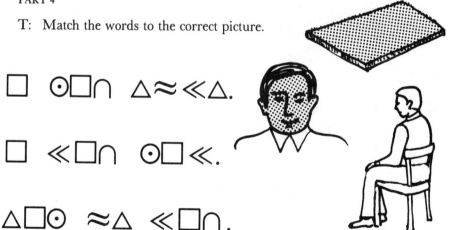

Sample Reactions

In the phonics lesson, the participant may have had any of the following reactions:

1. It was a challenge to try to remember the individual letter-sound relationships.
    Implication: The gamelike challenge of learning phonic skills should not be overlooked. There seems to be a natural fascination in learning codes like our alphabet, but students often want to discover relationships themselves rather than to be told. As instructor, you may want to devise discovery activities.

2. More drill on the recognition of individual letters would have been helpful. It would not have been dull. In fact, it would have been enjoyable.
    Implication: Once the students recognize a letter-sound relationship, they usually welcome the chance to practice it over and over. The instructor may think that the repetition is boring but the students usually will not. Perhaps your experience as student will have helped you to understand this.

3. An alphabet chart with picture clues to refer to would have been helpful. It would not be cheating; it would help learning.
    Implication: An alphabet chart posted in the room can be one of the most helpful aids you can give the students. They can refer to it as needed. Just seeing it each day will contribute valuable incidental learning opportunities.

4. It helped to have the instructor model the blending exercises.
    Implication: Imitating a model is an effective way of learning. Anytime you as instructor are introducing a new skill, try to demonstrate it first yourself. Remember how you felt as the student.

5. It helped to read along with the instructor.
    Implication: The joint reading activity allows the less-confident student the chance to practice reading with immediate feedback and little fear of embarrassment. Do not read ahead of your student. Make sure you are together and if possible let the student begin a word slightly before you.

6. It helped to write and say the letters at the same time.
    Implication: Most reading experts agree that learning is enhanced

whenever several modalities are used together. Whenever possible, students should be seeing, hearing, writing, and saying a word.

7. Some words could be recognized by sight without blending. It was annoying to have to blend words already known.

    Implication: In general, students should be allowed to read as fluently as they can. However, it is a good learning experience to blend some words that are already known since it can help the student get a grasp on the whole process of blending.

8. It was difficult to think about the meaning of what was being read when concentrating so hard on sounding out the words.

    Implication: There is a danger that the success of being able to sound out the words might become so rewarding in itself that meaning might be slighted. The instructor should work against this by asking questions about meaning after every sentence is completed.

THE SIGHT-WORD METHOD

Rationale

With the sight-word method students work with whole words, associating the written form of each word with its spoken form and its meaning. The method is based on two premises. The first is the idea that the whole word is the most natural language unit. Trying to get the student to work with any smaller unit (such as a syllable or a letter sound) would be unnatural and only cause unnecessary difficulties for the student and the teacher. The second premise is that the written form to be learned must always be meaningful. The students must always be "reading for meaning," not just pronouncing words. They would never be asked to drill nonsense syllables. Whenever possible, concrete aids would be used to help students to relate the written form to its meaning. Pictures are used liberally, objects in the classroom are labeled, and students are asked to act out the meaning of written words. These two premises lead to specific recommendations for instruction.

Treatment of Auditory Skills

Because of the use of the whole word as the basic unit, instructors would never ask students to learn letter sounds in isolation nor to blend them together into words. Students would be asked only to recognize sounds when used within real words as initial, final, or middle sounds. The following are typical instructions that might be given:

> Listen to words I say. Do they begin with the same or different sounds? /sun/, /sit/.
> Listen to the words I say. Raise your hand when I say a word that begins like *sun.* /ball/, /sit/, /car/.
> Listen to the words I say. Raise your hand when I say a word that begins with the letter *s.* /ball/, /sit/, /car/.

All the examples used in these auditory discrimination lessons would be real words. The students would never see or form letter combinations merely to practice sounds.

Treatment of Visual Skills

Students in a sight-word program would spend much time on activities designed to sharpen their visual discrimination skills. They might begin with seeing similarities and differences in pictures, abstract designs, letter patterns, and finally written words. Typical exercises would be like the following examples:

> Are these two words the same or different? Ball, book.
>
> Circle the word that is just like the first word.
>   book/   ball   goat   book   soon
>
> Draw a line around each word. Notice the shape it makes.
>   book   goat   sooner
>
> Trace the following word. Then copy it three or more times on the line.
>   book _____
>
> Fill in the missing letters.
>   book   __ook   boo__   b__ __k   b__ __ __

The problem of letter reversals would be handled as described under the phonic method, but word reversals and transpositions would be handled somewhat differently. Since blending skills are not developed in a sight-word program, there is no guarantee that the students will develop left-right sequencing habits. Visual discrimination exercises would be used that require students to focus on the beginning letter so that they will be certain to begin their scanning there. Also, they would be asked to discriminate words that differ only in letter sequence. The exercises would be like the following examples:

> Are the following words the same or different?
>   boat   coat
>   was   saw

> Circle the words that are the same as the first word.
>   stop/   spot   stop   sopt   stop   tops

Because of the reliance on visual discrimination skills, the instructor would begin with words that are obviously different and work toward those that are more similar in appearance. For example, an early lesson might introduce the following words:

> Pat   George   everyday   works

A primary activity to develop word recognition would simply be repetition. Words would be drilled on flash cards. Stories would be written in which the words are repeated many times. Here is an example using the words suggested above. Pictures would be used on each page.

> Pat
> George
> Pat and George
> Pat works everyday
> George works everyday
> Pat and George work everyday.

Treatment of Meaning

As has been stated previously, students of the sight method are expected always to be reading for meaning. They are encouraged to use the clues presented in pictures. New words are usually introduced and their meanings discussed before they appear in the story. In addition, a major portion of each lesson would be centered around a preparatory discussion during which the basic concepts of the reading passage would be introduced. The students would be encouraged to tell any part of their own experience that relates to these concepts. Usually some hints about the actual content of the story would be given to develop curiosity as a motivation for reading the story. This heavy emphasis on developing a meaning "set" would not be used in the early lessons of a phonic program because it would take away from the necessity to develop decoding skill.

Sample Lesson

This lesson is typical in design and content of the sight-word method. The reader might want to participate with a partner, taking turns acting as the student and the teacher. Refer to the Alphabet Code Chart (page 125).

STEP 1

T: (Points to the picture.) This is a picture of Tom. (Points to ≪⌈⊙.) This is the word *Tom*. Repeat after me, /Tom/.
S: /Tom/.
T: That's right, /Tom/.

STEP 2

T: (Points to the picture.) This is a picture of Molly. (Points to ⊙⌈∝∝⋚.) This is the word *Molly*. Repeat after me, /Molly/.
S: /Molly/.
T: That's right, /Molly/.

STEP 3

T: (Points to the picture.) This is a picture of a man sitting. (Points to △≈≪≪≈∩≅.) This is the word *sitting*. Repeat after me, /sitting/.
S: /sitting/.
T: That's right, /sitting/.

STEP 4

T: (Points to the picture.) This is a picture
of a bus. (Points to ◊≠△.) This says
/bus/. Repeat after me, /bus/.
S: /bus/.
T: That's right, /bus/.

$$\emptyset \ne \triangle$$

STEP 5

T: (Four sight words are presented one at
a time. The student is asked to say the
word. If any are missed, the pictures
shown in Steps 1 to 4 are presented
again as a review. In our regular alphabet, the four words are: Tom, Molly,
sitting, bus.)

$$\ll \lceil \odot$$
$$\odot \lceil \alpha \alpha \lessgtr$$
$$\triangle \approx \ll \ll \approx \cap \cong$$
$$\emptyset \ne \triangle$$

STEP 6

T: (Four review words presented. Since
only about five new words would be
presented in any one lesson, these
words are assumed to have been learned
in a previous lesson. In our regular
alphabet, the four words are: this, is, a,
on.)

$$\ll \emptyset \approx \triangle$$
$$\approx \triangle$$
$$\square$$
$$\lceil \cap$$

STEP 7

T: (Ask the student to read the story sheet that follows. For each two
lines, the following routine is used: read the lines together, then have
the student read them alone. *Note:* If this were a group activity, the
group would read together without the teacher. Then individuals
would be asked to read alone. In our regular alphabet, the story reads:
Tom. This is Tom. Molly. This is Molly. bus. This is a bus. Tom is
sitting on a bus. Molly is sitting on a bus.)

≪⌐⊙.

≪∅≈△ ≈△ ≪⌐⊙.

⊙⌐αα⑀.

≪∅≈△ ≈△ ⊙⌐αα⑀.

⟊≠△.

≪∅≈△ ≈△ ☐ ⟊≠△.

≪⌐⊙ ≈△ △≈≪≪≈∩≅ ⌐∩ ☐ ⟊≠△.

⊙⌐αα⑀ ≈△ △≈≪≪≈∩≅ ⌐∩ ☐ ⟊≠△.

STEP 8

T: (Ask the following questions to be answered orally by the students.)
    Who is this story about?
    What are Tom and Molly doing?
    Where are they?
    Where do you think they are going?
    What do you think may happen next in this story?

Sample Sight-Word Worksheet

PART 1

T: In each example circle the word that is the same as the first word.

≪⌐⊙　　　≪□)(　≪⌐⊙　≅⌐≪　≪≈∩

≪∅≈△　　≪∅≈△　≪∅)(⊙　≪∅≈∩

PART 2

T: Outline the following words. Notice the general shape.

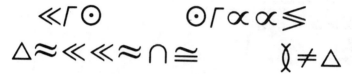

≪⌐⊙　　　⊙⌐∝∝≶

△≈≪≪≈∩≅　　　)(≠△

PART 3

T: Circle the shape that would fit the word at the beginning of the line.

)(≠△

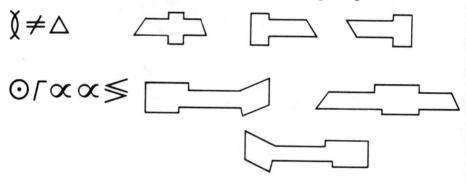

⊙⌐∝∝≶

PART 4

T: Fill in the missing letters in the following word. ≪⌐⊙

__⌐⊙　≪__⊙　≪____　≪⌐__

PART 5

T: Trace the word and then write it three more times on the line.

_____

⊙⌐∝∝≶

_____

△≈≪≪≈∩≅

_____

Sample Reactions

In the sight-word lesson, participants may have had the following reactions:

1. It was a challenge to remember what the individual words were.
    Implication: Each of the methods discussed in this chapter has its own
    challenge for the student and each can involve a natural self-moti-
    vation. As long as the students meet some initial success they will
    enjoy the task of memorizing words, especially if the words have
    some meaning in their daily lives.
2. It was natural to try to figure out what sounds individual letters have.
    Implication: Though sight-word teachers do not want students to
    learn individual sounds in isolation, students often want to do this.
    Again, a combination of some sight-word learning along with a
    phonics approach to the sounding out of simple, regularly spelled
    words can be a very effective way to teach initial reading.

3. Some similarities and differences could be spotted right away, but more repetition would have been helpful.

   Implication: Students often begin naturally to discover the regularities in words but often want a great deal of practice. As has been stressed before, the teacher may feel that the repetition is boring but the students seldom will because they are constantly testing out their new skills.

4. It would have helped to have the opportunity to see the spelling of other words.

   Implication: It is a good idea to encourage students to ask about other words not presented in the lesson that they would like to see. It will help them expand their vocabularies and involve them more actively in the learning process.

5. By relying on the general appearance of the words, it was often hard to remember what all the letters were.

   Implication: One drawback of the method is the lack of analysis of word structure. Students often confuse words with the same general shape. Since many of the most common words in English have similar shapes, this can be a real problem. Word-discrimination tasks and spelling activities should be introduced from the beginning to work against this danger.

6. It was easy to guess at words on the basis of a picture seen or discussion held prior to reading the story.

   Implication: The students should be using the context of the passage to help them read. They will only be hampered in their development of reading skill if their reliance on guessing keeps them from developing the habits of careful word analysis, which is necessary if they are to become independent readers. They need to use all their old and new knowledge about language in their reading tasks.

THE WORD-PATTERN METHOD

Rationale

The word-pattern method, like the phonic method, primarily teaches decoding skill and is based on the fact that English spelling patterns are predominantly regular. However, the advocates of this method state that the syllable is the basic language unit, disagreeing that isolated letter-sound associations should be learned. Letter sounds are dealt with only within whole syllables. In fact, adherents of the word-pattern method argue that it is useless to try to make the sound of the letters in isolation since they are always slightly different depending on the other letters that are around them. It is useless to learn to say /p/ when shown a letter *p* since it will never make exactly that sound in any word but will have a special variation best suited to blend in with the letters around it. The /p/ in *pan* is not the same as the /p/ in *pin* because the /p/ sound must be adapted to fit the *a* or the *i* that follows it. Word-pattern teachers feel that it is unnatural and unnecessarily difficult to teach the blending of individual sounds; therefore, the lessons deal directly with syllables.

Treatment of Auditory Skills

The auditory skills considered by the word-pattern method would deal only with sounds within syllables and would include the discrimination of syllables as the same or different, and the recognition of initial and final consonant sounds as the same or different. Rhyming is a skill of primary importance to the word-pattern method since it is the factor used to form the word families or basic patterns on which the method relies.

Typical exercises to develop auditory skills would be:

Listen to the words I say. Are they the same or different?

    ram   ram

    sat   cat

Raise your hand each time I say a word that begins like *sun*.

    sat   bus   run   such

Listen to the words I say. Do they rhyme?

    mad   sad

    rim   rack

    pot   pod

What word rhymes with *sat* and begins like *my?* [mat] (Note that letter sounds are never given in isolation, but always within words.)

Raise your hand whenever I say a word that rhymes with *sat*.

    bat   coat   man   mad   fit   cat   fat

Treatment of Visual Skills

Visual skills would be taught as much as possible at the level of the whole syllable and would center around the particular word patterns being taught. The distinguishing feature of visual skill development in this program would be the emphasis on developing facility in recognizing word patterns. Students might be asked to sort words according to pattern, complete missing elements in patterns, or recognize words that do not belong in a particular pattern group. The following are examples:

Sort the following words into three groups according to their spelling pattern:
        bad fan pig mad sad fig man dig can
Complete the missing elements to make the words fit the pattern.
        big   dig   ji__   r____
        pat   f__t   b__t   r____
Circle the word that does not belong in each group:
        dish   much   fish   wish
        mud   bud   job   dud

Treatment of Meaning

Words introduced in the early lessons of a word-pattern program are not chosen primarily for their meaningfulness to the students but rather on the basis of the particular word pattern being introduced. The choice often is even more limited than that of a phonic program because the phonic lesson would allow the known letter elements to be combined in any order, while the word-pattern lesson would use only the order of the patterns introduced. For example, in the phonics method, as soon as a student knows the letter sounds /a/, /m/, /n/, and /t/, they can be given a story with the words *am, man, mat, tan, an, Nan, at,* and *tat.* Both the beginning and ending consonants can be changed and used in various combinations. In a word-pattern lesson, however, the combinations are introduced one at a time. Students in a word-pattern program who had learned *pan* would not be expected to read *nap* on their own as a phonics reader would. So if the first lesson is on the *an* pattern, all the words end in *an,* with the exception of a few utility words introduced as sight words. The story would be quite singsongy, such as the following:

Dan is a man.
Dan ran.
Can Dan fan?
Dan can fan.
Dan can fan Nan.

The word-pattern reading book, like the phonics book, would severely limit pictures as clues to meaning since the students are being encouraged to use their recognition of word patterns alone. Also, the lessons would not begin with the lengthy introductions and concept discussions common to the sight-word method since the object is to teach the student to rely on the printed word as the source of meaning. Discussions and activities with concepts and vocabulary would follow the reading exercise since the instructor does want the students to realize that reading conveys meaning.

Sample Lesson

The following is a sample of a lesson using the word-pattern method approach, which provides an understanding of the roles of student and teacher in this kind of lesson. Refer to the Alphabet Code Chart (page 125).

STEP 1

T: These words are all in the /id/ family. (Point to ≈ ɔ.)   This says /id/. What does it say?

≈ ɔ

S: /id/.
T: That's right, /id/.

STEP 2

T: Let's say the rest of the words on this page. Repeat after me. (Point to ∅ ≈ ɔ.)   /hid/.

∅ ≈ ɔ

S: /hid/.
T: (Point to ⇋ ≈ ɔ.)   /kid/.

⇋ ≈ ɔ

S: /kid/.
T: (Point to △ ≈ ɔ.)   /Sid/.

△ ≈ ɔ

S: /Sid/.
T: (Point to ∝ ≈ ɔ.)   /lid/.

∝ ≈ ɔ

S: /lid/.

T: (Point to ⊙≈◯.)   /mid/.

S: /mid/.

STEP 3

T: Now I'll say some of the words on the list we just read and you finish the list. (Point to the first three words, one at a time, pronouncing each one. Then point to the last two and have the student say them. If unable to say the word, pronounce it again and ask the student to repeat it.)

STEP 4

T: Now I'll say a word and you point to it on the list. (Pronounce each word on the list in random order and have the student point to it. If the student is unable to find the correct word, point to it and repeat the word later in the sequence.)

STEP 5

T: Say the word I point to. (Point to the words on the list in random order. Point to each word at least twice.)

STEP 6

T: Now point to each word and tell me what it says.

STEP 7

T: (Point to ‖ ∅ Γ.) This says /who/. What does it say?

S: /who/.

T: That's right, /who/.

STEP 8

T: (Point to ≪ ∅ ∮.) This says /the/. What does it say?

S: /the/.

T: That's right, /the/.

STEP 9

T: (Point to ≈ ∩.) This says /in/. What does it say?

S: /in/.

T: That's right/in/.

STEP 10

T: (Point to □.) This says /a/. What does it say?
S: /a/.
T: That's right, /a/.

STEP 11

T: (Point to ᴑ≈ᴐ.) This says /did/. What does it say?
S: /did/.
T: That's right, /did/.

STEP 12

T: (For steps 12–17 refer to the word-pattern story that follows below. In our regular alphabet, the story reads: Who hid Sid? The kid did. The kid hid Sid. Who did? The kid hid Sid. The kid hid Sid in a lid.)

T: Now we will read a story. (Point to line 1 of the story). Read with me.

T & S: Who hid Sid?

T: Now you read alone.

S: Who hid Sid?

STEP 13

T: (Point to △≈○.) What does this say?
S: /Sid/.
T: That's right, /Sid/. Do you see it again in the story? Point to it every time you see it. (Student points to △≈○ in line 3, line 5, and line 6.)

STEP 14

T: (Repeat Step 13 for ∅≈○ and ≪∅ƒ.)

STEP 15

T: Now let's read together line 2.
T & S: /The kid did./
T: Now you read alone.
S: /The kid did./

STEP 16

T: (Repeat Step 15 for lines 3–6.)

STEP 17

T: Now read the whole story.

Sample Worksheet

PART 1

T: Match each word to a picture.

PART 2

T: Put the following words in three lines based on the pattern they use.

$\int\approx\circlearrowright$ $\pi\approx\cong$ $\therefore\square\cap$ $\therefore\approx\cong$

$\leftrightarrow\approx\cong$ $\propto\approx\circlearrowright$ $\int\approx\cong$ $\leftrightarrow\square\cap$

$\varnothing\approx\circlearrowright$ $\odot\square\cap$ $\circlearrowright\approx\circlearrowright$ $\infty\square\cap$

_____   _____   _____   _____

_____   _____   _____   _____

_____   _____   _____   _____

PART 3

T: Fill in the letters to make the words match the pictures.

$\ll\varnothing\int$ ___$\approx\circlearrowright$ $\varnothing\approx$___.

△≈◌'△ ____≈____.

PART 4

T: Write the words you hear me say. /hid/, /Sid/, /lid/, /kid/, /who/, /the/, /in/, and /a/.

1._____   2._____   3._____   4._____

5._____   6._____   7._____   8._____

Sample Reactions

In the word-pattern lesson, participants may have had the following reactions:

1. Learning to recognize patterns was challenging and enjoyable.
   Implication: The mastery of the word patterns is a type of discovery activity.
2. It helped to go through the exercises of seeing and writing words in pattern groups.
   Implication: Every time the students see the words grouped according to a spelling pattern, their ability to recognize the pattern later is strengthened. Pattern charts might be displayed in the classrooms to provide additional opportunities for this incidental learning. Also, the mechanical activity of actually writing out the words in pattern groups seems to help. Remember that learning is stronger when several modalities are used.
3. It was natural to try to remember individual letter sounds.

Implication: Although advocates of a word-pattern approach speak against the learning of letter sounds, it often seems that students want to use both sounding out and pattern approaches. The two methods seem to complement each other.

4. The language of the story seemed unnatural and singsongy.

   Implication: Students and teachers often find the sound of a pattern-based story strange, especially in the early lessons. They may be amused or annoyed but will seldom feel comfortable with it.

5. It was difficult to think about meaning when recognition of patterns was required. The story content had little importance anyway.

   Implication: As with the phonics approach, there is always the possibility that reading for meaning will be slighted with a pattern approach. Again, the instructor should guard against this by asking frequent questions about the content. The content, however, may still remain rather removed from the students' experience.

6. It was possible to remember some words by sight without reference to the pattern.

   Implication: Because some words are repeated often the students may simply be memorizing them. To make sure that the students are learning to use patterns, the instructor should constantly challenge them with pattern words they have not seen before.

THE LANGUAGE-EXPERIENCE METHOD

Rationale

Like the sight-word method, the language-experience method emphasizes meaning as a primary guide in selecting words for initial reading lessons. The materials, however, are generated in a unique way. Students orally tell the instructor something from their own experience, perhaps some basic information about themselves, their family, their job, or something they have seen or done. The instructor transcribes the students' words and reads them back. Then the instructor guides the students in reading their own passages. The words of the passages in turn become the raw material for other reading skill activities.

There is some controversy as to whether changes should be made in the student's language to make it more acceptable as written English. Some feel that no changes should be made since the student will most easily relate meaningfully to their own way of using language. Others feel that nonstandard language should not be reinforced in this way since ABE and developmental education students will need to learn to read and write standard English eventually and will only be handicapped by seeing nonstandard language in black and white. The whole matter of the proper way to transfer from everyday language to more formal written language is still an open question. However, many advocates of this method agree that clearly ungrammatical forms such as incomplete or run-on sentences or incorrect verb and pronoun forms should be corrected. Matters of style such as awkward phrasing or lack of variety in word choice and sentence structure need not be corrected.

Nonetheless, it is clear that words are more strictly limited with the language-experience method than they are with the sight-word method because with the latter method the authors of the stories can select the words and choose those easier to discriminate. They can structure the paragraphs to allow frequent repetition of the words being taught. The language-experience instructor must stick to what the student says. Often there will not be much repetition of the same words, and words very similar in configuration may be used. However, advocates of the method feel that since the words are the student's own, they will be easily recognized and will not need much repetition.

It is interesting to note that advocates of this method take the students' *idea* as the basic language unit—not the letter, syllable, or even the word. The student learns to recognize words as a part of his or her own idea.

Treatment of Auditory Skills

Like the sight-word instructor, the language-experience instructor will develop lessons about letter sounds using the words from the experience story. For example, if the student used the words *she, show,* and *ship,* the instructor could introduce other *sh* words and concentrate on the /sh/ sound by using drill cards, worksheets, games, and activities similar to those used by a phonics teacher. If the student used the words *had* and *bad,* the instructor might present a chart of *ad* words together with other practice materials, like those used by a word-pattern teacher.

While these examples might make this method look the most eclectic, it must be remembered that it is mainly a meaning-based system and does not present decoding skills in a way that is systematic and thorough enough to satisfy the advocate of a phonic or word-pattern method. The language-experience teacher feels that, when using the student's own words as examples, decoding skills can be acquired with very little drill.

Treatment of Visual Skills

The instructor begins with the student's own words when designing activities to sharpen visual skills. If the student is confusing *b* and *d* or reversing and transposing letters within words, exercises could be developed like those previously discussed. But this is not to be expected. Since the students know what they said, they will not be likely to misread the words. As they correctly read these words, they will be building good habits to use when reading unfamiliar materials.

The words of the story would be used in a great variety of sight-word drills, like those used by the sight-word teacher. The students would be collecting their own sets of word cards to use when they write down their own stories.

Treatment of Meaning

The language-experience method uses words of particular individual meaning to the student. This is the source of both strength and weakness. The use of this special class of words makes learning to recognize words easier since motivation is high and meaning immediately available. The student will also have occasion to use the words again, thus reinforcing them. However, the student may not be acquiring the basic sight vocabulary needed to read published materials. Students also may not become familiar with the language forms they will encounter in later reading or the variety of concepts they will need.

Sample Lesson

The sample lesson for the language-experience method is presented in a somewhat different way since participants will be generating their own materials.

STEP 1

Students orally tell the instructor something from personal experience in three or four simple sentences. It might be a self-descriptive report of current activities, past life, family and friends, interests and plans for the future, or something seen or heard; in short, it can be anything that the student wishes to relate.

STEP 2

The instructor writes down what the students have said. When longer passages are generated, a tape recorder may be useful. The instructor can transcribe it while the students are engaged in another activity. As students gain in spelling skill, they can begin to write down their own experiences in rough form with the instructor helping them later to perfect it.

STEP 3

The instructor places the written passage in front of the student and reads it back, pointing to each word as spoken. The teacher then asks the student if this is what was said, and makes any corrections suggested by the student.

STEP 4

The instructor goes back and reads the first line. The student is invited to read it. The teacher asks the student to read it alone. If any words in the first line appear elsewhere in the passage, the instructor asks the student to find them. The same procedure is repeated for each line. After each line is read, the student is asked to read the passage from the beginning.

STEP 5

The instructor points to individual words in the story and asks what they are. The student is asked to make a flash card (in code) for each word in the story. These cards can then be used for brief drills.

STEP 6

The instructor inspects the words in this story to see if there are any appropriate decoding exercises that can be drawn from them. Here are some suggested things to look for:

1. Regular spelling patterns that could generate a number of other useful, common words. For example, if the student used the word *had,* you could make a pattern page to teach other common *ad* words, such as *bad, sad, mad.*
2. Consonant sounds that are repeated in more than one word, especially more difficult ones, such as the digraphs *th, wh, sh,* and *ch.* Introduce students to this letter form on a blank letter card and have them think of other words that contain this sound. Help them spell out these words and add them to their flash cards.
3. Devise some sample blending exercises using the consonant sounds and a short vowel. Make up some visual discrimination exercises like those described for *b* and *d* problems and letter reversal and transposing problems, or for words with very similar configurations.
4. Words with common suffixes, such as *s, ed,* and *ing.* Make cards for these using blank letter cards and help the students add them to their flash cards and read the new words they have made.
5. Words that have the same sound spelled in different ways or that have the same letter making different sounds. Devise a chart listing the various pronunciations of letters to help the students remember letter-sound relationships. For example, *s* and *c* can both say /s/; /e/ can be written as *ee* or *ea.*

STEP 7

Have the students practice copying the words in their stories, in isolation and in sentences.

STEP 8

Have them make up new sentences using their words.

STEP 9

Give them dictations of words and sentences using their words.

Sample Reactions

In the language-experience lesson, participants may have had the following reactions:

1. It was a strange but satisfying feeling to see one's own words recorded in the unfamiliar code.

    Implication: It is often a thrilling experience for students the first time they see their own words in print. A tremendous amount of learning can be compressed into that one moment.

2. Remembering what was said and knowing from experience about the concepts that were described really helped when reading the passages.

    Implication: This is both a strength and a weakness of the language-experience approach. The flow of remembered meaning does permit the student to read more fluently and make more use of rudimentary reading skills. However, it may provide something of a crutch that will keep the student from developing decoding skills for later independent reading. The instructor should include many other activities to strengthen decoding skill.

3. There was a certain curiosity in breaking the alphabet code.

    Implication: The students should be encouraged to request words and should be exposed to words with letters and word patterns similar to the ones they have used in their stories.

4. It was enjoyable to read one's own stories, but it wasn't the same experience as reading "real" books.

    Implication: Adult students may become impatient with the language-experience tasks because they want to read the sorts of everyday reading matter they associate with literate people. Therefore, it is probably important to begin to introduce the basic sight words and decoding skills they will need more systematically, not just on the basis of chance occurrence in the experience stories. Again, it is advisable to use a combination of all four methods discussed in this chapter in order to bring the student to literacy in the most efficient way.

APPLICATION EXERCISES

Four contrasting approaches to the teaching of beginning reading have been described in this chapter. As a way of summarizing the similarities and differences among these approaches, the following application exercises are provided.

Exercise A

Next to each of the following statements, indicate which method the statement seems to be advocating. Sometimes more than one method may be a possible answer. Use the following symbols for your answers

> PH = Phonics Method
> SW = Sight-Word Method
> WP = Word-Pattern Method
> LE = Language-Experience Method

The correct responses and brief explanations are listed in the answer key that follows Exercise B.

_____ 1. Decoding skill is changing printed letters into sounds. This is what reading essentially is.

_____ 2. Concept development is an important part of the lesson plans. Concepts are presented at the beginning of each lesson.

_____ 3. I also felt that the words elicited from students by their teachers were the best sight vocabulary ever devised.

_____ 4. Words should be repeated frequently if students are to remember them.

_____ 5. This method introduces the student first to words like *man, ran,* and *pan,* and lets him discover for himself that the *an* sound and its spelling are constant.

_____ 6. The reading materials for new readers should use their own words, the words they would like to know. They begin by seeing their own speech written down.

_____ 7. With the exception of a handful of special words, every story should contain only the letter sounds that have been taught at any point.

_____ 8. Thus, starting with the simplest patterns and gradually progressing to more complex patterns, the program introduces more and more patterns from which the student can draw his own generalizations.

Exercise B

Read the following examples of instructions. They have been adapted from various teacher's manuals. Indicate which method is being used. Again, more than one method may be appropriate. Use the same abbreviations as you did in Exercise A. An answer key follows.

————— 1. Direct their attention to the picture in the reader and ask, "What do you think the story will be about?"

————— 2. Take out the letter cards. Present them one at a time to the students. They should give the sound of the letter as soon as you point to it.

————— 3. Present the word *cat*. Say, "Now we will blend our letter sounds to make a new word. As I point to each letter, make its sound."

————— 4. Write these words on the board in a column: Dan, can, man, pan, ran, tan.

————— 5. We strongly recommend that you use the following three steps: (a) picture reading, (b) silent reading and talking it over, (c) oral reading.

————— 6. Take out the flash cards for review words. Present them one at a time to the students. Accept only immediate recall as a correct answer.

————— 7. Take the student's story and find words that are alike, words that begin alike, and words that begin like their names.

————— 8. Have the students read the following passage: I see Tat. I see the mat. I see the rat. I see the rat at the mat.

————— 9. Have the student dictate to you a passage about the picture.

————— 10. First, present the pattern chart of *ot* words. Practice reading these words in various orders. Ask students to spell them orally, by letter names, then turn to the reading passage for this lesson.

————— 11. Begin by introducing the new sound-symbol relationships. Practice blending these new elements into simple words. Then introduce the reading passage.

Answer Key to Exercise A

__PH__ 1. An important step in phonics instruction is to associate sounds with the letters used to represent them.

__SW__ 2. Only the sight-word teacher would spend a great deal of initial time on concept development.

__LE__ 3. The language-experience teacher uses the student's own words as sight words.

__SW__ 4. The sight-word method expects readers to learn to recognize words by encountering them repeatedly in meaningful contexts.

__WP__ 5. This is a typical pattern list used in the word-pattern method. Also, the word-pattern method tends to encourage discovery.

__LE__ 6. The rationale for the language-experience is that reading should build on the language the adult is already using.

PH,WP 7. Both of these methods that emphasize decoding introduce some sight words, but most of the words must reflect the sounds being taught up to that point.

__WP__ 8. The word pattern approach helps students build a repertoire of patterns to use as a framework in recognizing new words.

Answer Key to Exercise B

__SW__ 1. Again, it is only the sight-word teacher who teaches beginning readers to rely on picture clues in reading.

__PH__ 2. A phonics teacher asks the students to remember letter sounds.

__PH__ 3. This is an example of a blending exercise used by phonics teachers.

__WP__ 4. In the word pattern method, learning is felt to occur when students see, write, and read words in patterns.

__SW__ 5. This is a typical sequence of activities for a sight-word instructor emphasizing discussion of meaning throughout.

__SW__ 6. This teacher is asking for immediate memory of whole words; no sounding is allowed.

__LE__   7. The language-experience method does teach word-study skills but only as they are indicated by the words chosen by the student.

__WP__   8. This emphasis on patterns identifies the word-pattern method.

__LE__   9. This is the method that is concerned with transcribing the student's own words.

__WP__   10. The use of a pattern chart identifies the word-pattern approach. Also, the spelling of words by letter names is typical of this method. Also note that this attention to word analysis comes before the reading passage.

__PH__   11. Only the phonics teacher deals with blending isolated sounds.

SUGGESTIONS FOR FURTHER READING

The topic of beginning reading instruction for adult students is discussed in an increasing number of articles and publications including Bernstein (1980), Boraks and Richardson (1981), Hansen and Feinberg (1982), Haverson and Haynes (1982), Hoffman (1980), Keefe (1982), Malieky and Norman (1982), Mattran (1981), Milligan (1982), Peters (1981), Pope (1975), Sainz and Biggins (1980), Scales and Biggs (1976), and Wyatt (1980). Some specific techniques are described in Cohen (1981), Crutchfield (1981), Finlay (1981), Meyer (1982), and Richardson (1981).

BIBLIOGRAPHY
INDEX

BIBLIOGRAPHY

ABE teaching/learning management system. Final report. Indianapolis: Indiana State Department of Public Instruction, Division of Adult and Community Education, 1981. (ERIC Document Reproduction Service No. ED 211 669)

Adult education program guide. Office of Instructional Services, Adult Education Section, Department of Education, State of Hawaii, Publication #TAC 72-407, 1975.

Aker, G. Learning and the older adult. *Education for older citizens.* Tallahassee: Florida State University, June, 1971.

Aker, G. Cognition and aging: Verbal learning memory and problem solving. In C. Eisdorfer & M. P. Lawton (Eds.), *The psychology of adult development and aging.* Washington, D.C.: American Psychological Association, 1973.

Amidon, E., & Hunter, E. *Improving teaching.* New York: Holt, Rinehart & Winston, 1966.

Andersen, D. G. Learning and modification of attitudes in pre-retirement education. *Adult Leadership,* 1969, *18*(9), 381–82.

Anderson, R. C. Learning in discussion: A resume of authoritarian-democratic studies. *Harvard Educational Review,* 1959, *29*(3), 201–15.

Artley, A. S. Reading instruction and cognitive development. *Elementary School Journal,* 1977, *77,* 203–11.

Aspects of educational assessment. Princeton, N.J.: Educational Testing Service Center for Statewide Educational Assessment, 1975.

Axford, R. W. *Adult education: The open door to lifelong learning.* Indiana, Pa.: A. G. Halldin, 1980.

Barney, A. S. *Characteristics and educational needs of adult undergraduate students at the University of Oklahoma.* Doctoral dissertation, University of Oklahoma, 1972.

Basowitz, H., & Korchin, S. J. Age differences in the perception of closure. *Journal of Abnormal and Social Psychology,* 1957, *54,* 93–97.

Berg, J., & Wallace, U. A. *A selected bibliography of functional literacy materials for adult learners,* 1980. (ERIC Document Reproduction Service No. 199 551)

Beris, C. *A comparison of the readability of selected instructions, publications, and forms commonly used by adults and the minimum literacy level as defined by the United States Office of Education,* 1982. (ERIC Document Reproduction Service No. ED 217 372)

Berne, E. *Games people play.* New York: Grove Press, 1964.

Bergquist, W. H., & Phillips, S. R. *A Handbook for faculty development.* Washington, D.C.: Council for the Advancement of Small Colleges, 1975.

Bernstein, J. *People, words and change.* Literacy volunteer handbook. 1980. (ERIC Document Reproduction Service No. ED 198 310)

Bilash, I., & Zube, J. D. The effects of age on factorially "pure" mental abilities. *Journal of Gerontology,* 1960, *15,* 175–82.

Birren, J. E. *Handbook of aging and the individual.* Chicago: The University of Chicago Press, 1959.

Birren, J. E. *The psychology of aging.* Englewood Cliffs, N.J.: Prentice-Hall, 1964.

Birren, J. E. Adult capacities to learn. In R. G. Kuhlen (Ed.), *Psychological background of adult education.* Syracuse, N.Y.: Syracuse University Publications in Continuing Education, 1970.

Birren, J. E. A summary. In L. F. Jarvik, C. Eisdorfer, & J. E. Blum (Eds.), *Intellectual functioning in adults.* New York: Springer, 1973.

Birren, J. E. & Shock, N. W. Age changes in rate and level of visual dark adaptation. *Journal of Applied Physiology,* 1950, *2,* 407–11.

Birren, J. E., & Woodruff, D. S. A life-span perspective for education. *New York University Education Quarterly,* 1973, *4*(4), 25–31.

Bischof, L. J. *Adult psychology.* New York: Harper & Row, 1976.

Bloom, B. S. *Taxonomy of educational objectives.* New York: David McKay, 1956.

Boaz, R. L. *Participation in adult education: Final report, 1975.* Washington, D.C.: National Center for Educational Statistics, 1978.

Boraks, N., & Richardson, J. *Teaching the adult beginning reader: Designing research based reading instructional strategies.* 1981. (ERIC Document Reproduction Service No. ED 216 329)

Boshier, R. Motivational orientations of adult education participants: A factor analytic exploration of Houle's typology. *Adult Education,* 1971, *21,* 3–26.

Boshier, R. Education participation and dropout: A theoretical model. *Adult Education,* 1973, *23,* 255–82.

Boshier, R. Motivational orientation revisited: Life-space motivation and the education participation scale. *Adult Education,* 1977, *27,* 89–115.

Boshier, R. Effects of fees on clientele characteristics and participation in adult education. *Adult Education,* 1979, *29,* 151–69.

Botwinick, J. *Cognitive processes in maturity and old age.* New York: Springer, 1967.

Botwinick, J. *Aging and behavior.* New York: Springer, 1973.

Bradley, R. C. Structuring questions. *Arizona Teacher,* 1966, *54,* 14–15.

Branden, N. *The psychology of self-esteem.* New York: Bantam Books, 1971.

Brockner, J. The effects of self-esteem, success/failure, and self-consciousness on task performance. *Journal of Personality and Social Psychology,* 1979, *37,* 1732–41.

Brookover, W. B., Thomas, S., & Paterson, A. Self-concept of ability and school achievement. *Sociology of Education,* 1964, *34,* 271–78.

Broverman, I. K., Broverman, D. M., Clarkson, F. E., Rosenkrantz, P. S., & Vogel, S. R. Sex-role stereotype and clinical judgments of mental health. *Journal of Consulting and Clinical Psychology,* 1970, *34,* 1–7.

Brundage, D. H., & Mackeracher, D. *Adult learning principles and their application to program planning.* Ontario, Canada: Ontario Institute for Studies in Education, 1980.

Brunner, E., Wilder, D. S., Kirchner, C., & Newberry, J. S. *An overview of adult education research.* Chicago: Adult Education Association/United States of America, 1959.

Buhler, C. The curve of life as studied in biographies. *Journal of Applied Psychology,* 1935, *19,* 405–09.

Burgess, P. Reasons for participation in group educational activities. *Adult Education,* 1971, *22*(1), 3–29.

Burkhart, R. C. *Spontaneous and deliberate ways of learning.* Scranton, Pa.: International Textbook Company, 1962.

Buros, O. K. *The eighth mental measurements yearbook.* Highland Park, N.J.: The Gryphon Press, 1978.

Canestrari, R. E., Jr. Paced or self-paced learning in young and elderly adults. *Journal of Gerontology,* 1963, *18,* 165–68.

Carner, R. L. Levels of questioning. *Education,* 1963, *83*(9), 546–50.

Checklist for evaluating adult basic education reading materials. *Journal of Reading,* 1981, *24*(8), 701–06.

Clinic to Improve University Teaching. *Working definitions of some technical skills of teaching.* Amherst, Mass.: University of Massachusetts, 1975.

Cohen, J. *A reading and writing program using language-experience methodology among adult ESL students in a basic education program.* Washington, D.C.: Office of Vocational and Adult Education, 1981. (ERIC Document Reproduction Service No. 213 914)

Comfort, R. W. Higher adult education program: A model. *Adult Leadership,* 1974, *11*(7), 6–8, 25–29, 32.

Cook, W. D. *Adult literacy education in the United States.* Newark, N.J.: International Reading Association, 1977.

Cotton, W. E. *On behalf of adult education.* Boston: Center for the Study of Liberal Education for Adults, 1968.

Cross, J. S., & Nagle, J. M. Teachers talk too much. *English Journal,* 1969, *58*(9), 1362-65.

Cross, K. P. *Beyond the open door: New students to higher education.* San Francisco: Jossey-Bass, 1971.

Cross, K. P. *Adults as learners.* San Francisco: Jossey-Bass, 1982.

Crutchfield, J. E. *Using LEA to improve adult reading skills,* 1981. (ERIC Document Reproduction Service No. ED 217 153)

Dale, E., & Chall, J. S. A formula for predicting readability. *Educational Research Bulletin,* 1948, *27,* 11-20, 37-54.

Darkenwald, G. G., & Merriam, S. B. *Adult education: Foundations of practice.* New York: Harper & Row, 1982.

Demchik, M. J., & Demchik, V. C. How inquiry may set the structure for learning. *Science Education,* 1970 *54*(1), 1-4.

Dennis, L. E. The other end of Sesame Street. In G. Kerry Smith (Ed.), *New teaching new learning.* San Francisco: Jossey-Bass, 1971.

DeSanctis, V. The adult education legislation: 1964-1979. *Adult literacy and basic education.* 1980, *3*(4), 245-53.

Dickenson, G. *Teaching adults: A handbook for instructors.* Toronto: New Press, 1973.

Dickenson, G., & Rubidge, N. A. Testing knowledge about adult education. *Adult Education,* 1973, *23*(4), 283-97.

Doherty, P. A., & Schmidt, M. R. Sex-typing and self-concept in college women. *Journal of College Student Personnel,* 1978, *19,* 493-97.

Domey, R. G., McFarland, R. A., & Chadwick, E. Dark adaptation as a function of age and time: II. A derivation. *Journal of Gerontology,* 1960, *15,* 267-79.

Drennan, A. P. Adult basic education and English as a second language: A critique. In E. J. Boone, R. W. Shearon, & E. E. White (Eds.), *Serving personal and community needs through adult education.* San Francisco: Jossey-Bass, 1980.

Easy adult reading materials: A bibliography of bibliographies. *Reading Quarterly,* 1973, *13,* 43-47.

Eichorn, D. H. The Institute of Human Development Studies. Berkeley and Oakland. In L. F. Jarvik, C. Eisdorfer, & J. E. Blum (Eds.), *Intellectual functioning in adults.* New York: Springer, 1973.

Eisdorfer, C. Verbal learning and response time in the aged. *Journal of Genetic Psychology,* 1965, *152,* 15-22.

Entine, A. D. Mid-life counseling: Prognosis and potential. *Personnel and Guidance Journal,* November 1976, *55*(3), 112-14.

Erikson, E. H. *Childhood and society.* New York: W. W. Norton & Co., 1950.

Finlay, J. Instruction for illiterates: The initial teaching alphabet. *Australian Journal of Adult Education,* 1981, *21*(1), 15–18.

Fitts, W. H. *The self-concept and behavior.* Nashville, Tenn.: Dede Wallace Center, 1972.

Florida Department of Education. *A review of physiological and psychological changes in aging and their implications for teachers of adults.* Tallahassee: Department of Adult Education, Florida State University, 1973.

Foulds, G. A., & Raven, J. C. Normal changes in the mental abilities of adults as age advances. *Journal of Mental Science,* 1948, *94,* 133–42.

Fraenkel, J. Ask the right questions. *Clearinghouse,* March 1966, *40*(7), 397–400.

Fristae, J. W. Questions, questions, questions. *School and Community,* 1964, *50,* 15.

Fromm, E. *Escape from freedom.* New York: Holt, Rinehart and Winston, 1941.

Gantt, W. N. Questioning for thinking. *Reading Teacher,* October 1970, *24*(1), 12–16.

Geist, H. *The psychological aspects of the aging process with sociological implications.* St. Louis, Mo.: Warren H. Green, 1968.

Gilbert, J. C. Age changes in color matching. *Journal of Gerontology,* 1957, *12,* 210–15.

Glass, C. J., & Harshberger, R. F. The full-time, middle-aged adult student in higher education. *Journal of Higher Education,* 1974, *45*(3), 211–17.

Glasser, W. *Schools without failure.* New York: Harper & Row, 1968.

Goffe, L., & Deane, N. Questioning our questions. *College Composition and Communication,* 1974, *25,* 284–91.

Gordon, C., & Kenneth, G. *The self in social interaction.* New York: Wiley & Sons, 1968.

Gornick, V., & Morgan, B. K. *Woman in sexist society: Studies in power and powerlessness.* New York: Basic Books, 1971.

Gould, R. Adult life stages: Growth toward self-tolerance. *Psychology Today,* February 1975, 74–78.

Granick, S., & Riedman, A. S. Educational experience and the maintenance of intellectual functioning by the aged: An overview. In L. F. Jarvik, C. Eisdorfer, & J. E. Blum (Eds.), *Intellectual functioning in adults.* New York: Springer, 1973.

Grede, J., & Friedlander, J. Adult basic education in community colleges. *Junior College Research Review,* August 1981.

Griffith, F. *A handbook for the observation of teaching and learning.* Midland, Mich.: Pendell, 1973.

Groisser, P. *How to use the fine art of questioning.* New York: Teachers Practical Press, 1974.

Gross, R. *The lifelong learner.* New York: Simon and Schuster, 1977.

Grotelueschen, A. D. Program evaluation. In A. B. Knox (Ed.), *Developing, administering and evaluating adult education.* San Francisco: Jossey-Bass, 1980.

Grotelueschen, A. D., Gooter, D. D., & Knox, A. B. *Evaluation in adult education: How and why.* Danville, Ill.: Interstate Printers and Publishers, 1976.

Guilford, J. P. *Psychometric methods.* New York: McGraw-Hill, 1954.

Gunning, R. *The technique of clear writing* (Rev. ed.). New York: McGraw-Hill, 1968.

Guth, S. K., Eastman, A. A., & McNelis, J. F. Lighting requirements for older workers. *Illuminating Engineering,* 1956, *51,* 656–60.

Guthrie, J. T. Research: Invalidity of reading tests. *Journal of Reading,* 1981, *25*(3), 300–02.

Haines, D. B., & McKeachie, J. W. Cooperative vs. competitive discussion methods in teaching introductory psychology. *Journal of Educational Psychology,* 1967, *58*(6), 386–90.

Hambleton, R. K., & Gorth, W. P. *Criterion-referenced testing: Issues and application.* Amherst: University of Massachusetts School of Education, 1971.

Hand, S. E. What it means to teach older adults. In A. H. Hendrickson (Ed.), *A manual on planning educational programs for older adults.* Tallahassee: Department of Adult Education, Florida State University, 1973.

Hansen, C. L., & Feinberg, P. *Which words shall they learn.* 1982. (ERIC Document Reproduction Service No. ED 216 314)

Harris, A. J. *Some new developments in readability.* Paper presented at the International Reading Association World Congress on Reading, Vienna, Austria, August 1974. (ERIC Document Reproduction Service No. ED 094 344)

Harris, T. A. *I'm o.k.—you're o.k.* New York: Harper & Row, 1967.

Harrison, A. F., & Bamson, R. M. *Styles of thinking: Strategies for asking questions, making decisions and solving problems.* Garden City, N.Y.: Anchor Press, 1982.

Haverson, W. W., & Haynes, J. L. *ESL/literacy for adult learners. Language in education: Theory and practice.* No. 49. Washington, D.C.: National Institute of Education, 1982. (ERIC Document Reproduction Service No. ED 217 703)

Havighurst, R. J. *Developmental tasks and education.* New York: David McKay, 1972.

Havighurst, R. J., & Orr, B. *Adult education and adult needs.* Boston: Center for the Study of Liberal Education for Adults, 1956.

Hernes, J. M. *An examination of the literature on criterion-referenced and computer-assisted testing.* Boston University School of Education, Department of

Educational Media and Technology, 1975. (ERIC Document Reproduction Service No. ED 116 633)

Hoffman, L. M. ABE reading instruction: Give them something to read. *Community College Review,* 1980, *8*(1), 32–37.

Honzik, M. P., & MacFarlaine, J. W. Personality development and intellectual functioning from 21 months to 40 years. In L. F. Jarvik, C. Eisdorfer, & J. Blum (Eds.), *Intellectual functioning in adults.* New York: Springer, 1973.

Houle, C. O. *The inquiring mind.* Madison: University of Wisconsin Press, 1961.

Huberman, M. Looking at adult education from the perspective of the adult life cycle. *International Review of Education,* 1974, *20*(2), 117–36.

Hudspeth, M. C. Teach remedial mathematics at our university. *Journal of General Education,* 1978, *30,* 117–28.

Hunkins, F. P. *Questioning strategies and techniques.* Boston: Allyn and Bacon, 1972.

Hunkins, F. P. *Involving students in questioning.* Boston: Allyn & Bacon, 1976.

Hyman, R. T. *Strategic questioning.* Englewood Cliffs, N.J.: Prentice-Hall, 1979.

Jarvik, L. F., Eisdorfer, C., & Blum, J. E. (Eds.). *Intellectual functioning in adults.* New York: Springer, 1973.

Jensen, G. Developing a theory of adult learning. In I. Lorge, G. Jensen, L. Bradford, M. Bumbaum (Eds.), *Adult education theory and method: Adult learning.* Washington, D.C.: Adult Education Association of the U.S.A., 1963.

Johnson, M. S., & Kress, R. A. *Informal reading inventories.* Reading Aids Series #2. Newark, Del.: International Reading Association, 1965. (ERIC Document Reproduction Service No. ED 072 437)

Jones, H. E., & Conrad, H. S. The growth and decline of intelligence. *General Psychological Monograph,* 1973, *13,* 223–98.

Jung, C. G. *Modern man in search of a soul.* New York: Harcourt, Brace & World, Inc., 1933.

Jung, C. G. *The portable Jung.* (J. Campbell, Ed.). New York: Viking Press, 1971.

Kaiser, A. *Questioning techniques.* Pomona, Cal.: Hunter House, 1979.

Keefe, D. Adult disabled readers: Instructional strategies to improve comprehension. *Reading World,* 1982, *21*(4), 320–25.

Kidd, J. R. *How adults learn.* New York: Association Press, 1973.

Kimmel, D. C. *Adulthood and aging.* New York: John Wiley and Sons, 1974.

Klagsbrien, F. *How to pass high school equivalency examinations.* New York: Cowles Educational Corporation, 1967.

Klare, G. R. Assessing readability. *Reading Research Quarterly,* 1974–1975, *10,* 62–102.

Klare, G. R., & Buck, B. *Know your reader.* New York: Heritage House, 1954.

Klevins, C. (Ed.). *Materials & methods in adult & continuing education.* Canoga Park, Cal.: Klevens Publications, 1982.

Knowles, M. S. Issues in adult learning psychology. *Adult Leadership,* 1974, *22*(9), 300–16.

Knowles, M. S. *Self-directed learning.* New York: Association Press, 1975.

Knowles, M. S. *The adult learner: A neglected species.* Houston: Gulf Publishing Co., 1978.

Knowles, M. S. *The modern practice of adult education.* New York: Association Press, 1980.

Knox, A. *Helping adults to learn.* U.S., Educational Resources Information Center, 1974. (ERIC Document Reproduction Service No. ED 103 670)

Knox, A. *Adult development and learning.* San Francisco: Jossey-Bass, 1977.

Knox, A., & Sjogren, D. Research on adult learning. *Adult Education,* 1965, *15,* 133–37.

Kohlberg, L. Stages and aging in moral development—some speculations. *The Gerontologist,* 1973, *13*(4), 497–502.

Konig, J. Pitch discrimination and age. *Acta Oto-Laryngologica,* 1957, *68,* 473–89.

Korman, A. K. Self-esteem variable in vocational choice. *Journal of Applied Psychology,* 1966, *50,* 479–86.

Kuhlen, R. G. Motivational changes during the adult years. In Raymond G. Kuhlen (Ed.), *Psychological backgrounds of adult education.* Syracuse, N.Y.: Syracuse University Publications in Continuing Education, 1970.

LaBenne, V., & Greene, B. *Educational implications of self-concept theory.* Pacific Palisades, Cal.: Goodyear Publishing Co., 1969.

Ladas, H., & Osti, L. Asking questions: A strategy for teachers. *The High School Journal,* 1972, *4,* 48–52.

Lageman, J. The delicate art of asking questions. *Reader's Digest,* June 1965, *50,* 87–91.

Lalanne, J. Attack by questions. *Psychology Today,* 1975, *9,* 134.

Lamarre, P. *Resources: A guide for using published materials in adult literacy programs.* Instructional Concept Guide No. 11. University of Georgia, Athens, Georgia, 1975. (ERIC Document Reproduction Service No. ED 120 362)

Leonard, A. Developing print materials in Mexico for people who do not read. *Educational Broadcasting International,* 1980, *13*(4), 168–73.

Lorge, I. The influence of the test upon the nature of mental decline as a function of age. *Journal of Educational Psychology,* 1936, *27,* 100–10.

Lorge, I., Jensen, G., Bradford, L. P., & Birnbaum, M. The adult learner. In C.

Verner & T. White (Eds.), *Adult education theory and methods* (Vol. 4). Washington, D.C.: Adult Education Association of the U.S.A., 1963.

Loughlin, R. On questioning. *Educational Forum,* 1961, *25*(4), 481–82.

Lunneborg, P. W., Olch, D. R., & de Wolf, V. Prediction of college performance in older students. *Journal of Counseling Psychology,* 1974, *21*(3), 215–21.

Lyman, H. B. *Test scores and what they mean.* Englewood Cliffs, N.J.: Prentice-Hall, 1971.

McCabe, R. H., & Skidmore, S. The literacy crisis and American education. *Junior College Research Review,* Spring 1982, 1–6.

McClusky, H. The coming of age of lifelong learning. *Journal of Research and Development in Education,* 1974, *7*(4), 97–107.

McFarland, R. A., & Fisher, M. B. Alterations in dark adaptation as a function of age. *Journal of Gerontology,* 1963, *18,* 267–70.

Malieky, G., & Norman, C. A. Reading strategies of adult illiterates. *Journal of Reading,* 1982, *25*(8), 731–35.

Malmquist, E. *Developing reading ability—A worldwide challenge: The present situation and an outlook for the future.* 1981. (ERIC Document Reproduction Service No. ED 208 344)

Maltz, M. *Psycho-cybernetics.* Englewood Cliffs, N.J.: Prentice-Hall, 1960.

Mangione, A. How to train students and teachers to ask questions. *English Education,* 1972, *4,* 48–52.

Manson, G., & Clegg, A. A. Classroom questioning: Keys to children's thinking. *Peabody Journal of Education,* 1970, *47*(5), 302–07.

Maslow, A. *Motivation and personality.* New York: Harper & Row, 1954.

Mason, J. You can ask creative questions. *Nation's Business,* 1958, *46,* 84–87.

Mattran, K. J. *Breaking through the decoding barrier: A case study in adult literacy.* 1981. (ERIC Document Reproduction Service No. ED 203 131)

Melrose, J., Welsh, O. L., & Luterman, D. M. Auditory responses in selected elderly men. *Journal of Gerontology,* 1955, *10,* 424–28.

Mercier, L. Y. (Ed.) *Outlook for the 80's: Adult literacy.* Washington, D.C.: Department of Education, Basic Skills Improvement Program, 1981. (ERIC Document Reproduction Service No. ED 211 701)

Meyer, V. Prime-o-tec: A successful strategy for adult disabled readers. *Journal of Reading,* 1982, *25*(6), 512–15.

Miles, W. R. Psychological aspects of aging. In E. V. Cowdry & R. Kastenbaum (Eds.), *Problems of aging: Biological and medical aspects* (Rev. ed.). Salem, N.H.: Ayer, 1979.

Milligan, B. Literate at last—You "can" teach an old dog. *Australian Journal of Reading,* 1982, *5*(1), 24–29.

Montieth, M. K. Readability formulas. *Journal of Reading,* 1976, *19,* 604–07.

Moustakes, C. (Ed.) *The self: Explorations in personal growth*. New York: Harper & Row, 1956.

Murphy, G. *Psychological needs of adults: A symposium by Gardner Murphy and Raymond Kuhlen*. Chicago: Center for the Study of Liberal Education for Adults, 1955.

Nafriger, D. H. *Tests of functional adult literacy: An evaluation of currently available instruments*. Portland, Ore.: Northwest Regional Education Laboratory, 1975.

Neugarten, B. L. *Personality in middle and later life*. New York: Atherton Press, 1964.

Neugarten, B. L. *Middle age and aging*. Chicago: The University of Chicago Press, 1968.

Neugarten, B. L. Personality changes during the adult years. In R. G. Kuhlen (Ed.), *Psychological backgrounds of adult education*. Syracuse, N.Y.: Syracuse University Publications in Continuing Education, 1970.

Neugarten, B. L. The future and the young-old. *The Gerontologist*, 1975, *15*(1), 4–9.

O'Brien, R. L. *Books for adult new readers*. Cleveland, Oh.: George Gund Foundation, 1980. (ERIC Document Reproduction Service No. ED 201 738)

Olmo, B. M. Questioning: Heart of social studies. *Social Education*, 1969, *33*(8), 949–52.

Olmo, B. M. Focus on questioning. *Journal of Teacher Education*, Winter 1970, *21*(4), 504–08.

Owens, W. A. Age of mental abilities: A longitudinal study. *Genetic Psychology Monographs*. 1953, *68*, 3–54.

Owens, W. A., Jr. Age and mental abilities: A second adult follow-up. *Journal of Educational Psychology*. 1966, *67*, 311–25.

Pankowski, M. L. Teachers of adults will. *Journal of Extension*. September/October 1975, *13*, 7–13.

Payne, S. *The art of asking questions* (Rev. Ed.). Princeton, N.J.: Princeton University Press, 1980.

Peters, V. An ambulance emergency: Learning to read. *Phi Delta Kappa*, 1981, *62*(9), 668–69.

Pope, H. M. Current practices in the teaching of beginning reading. In John B. Carroll & Jean S. Chall (Eds.), *Toward a literate society*. New York: McGraw-Hill, 1975.

Potter, R. The art of questioning in the literature lesson. *Reading Teacher*, 1969, *22*(5), 423–25.

Potter, T. C., & Quenneth, R. *Informal reading diagnosis: A practical guide for the classroom teacher*. Englewood Cliffs, N.J.: Prentice-Hall, 1973.

Pressey, S. L., & Kuhlen, R. G. *Psychological development through the life span.* New York: Harper & Brothers, 1957.

Purkey, W. *Self-concept and school achievement.* Englewood Cliffs, N.J.: Prentice-Hall, 1970.

Putnam, J. F., & Chrisman, W. D. *Standard terminology of instructional content, resources and processes.* Washington, D.C.: U.S. Government Printing Office, 1967.

Ratteray, J. D. *Testing of cultural groups: A paradigmatic analysis of the literature on testing and a proposal.* Santa Monica, Cal.: Rand, 1975. (ERIC Document Reproduction Service No. ED 133 371)

Reisman, D. Asking and answering. *Journal of Business,* 1956, *29,* 225–36.

Richardson, J. S. Language experience for adult beginning readers: Sometimes it works. *Lifelong learning: The adult years,* 1981, *4*(8), 72–13.

Richardson, R. C., Martens, K. J., & Fisk, E. C. *Functional literacy in the community college setting.* AAHE/ERIC/Higher Education Research No. 3, 1981. Washington, D.C.: American Association for Higher Education, 1981.

Roehl, J. E. Improving the self-concept of reentry women students: Techniques and principles. *Lifelong Learning: The Adult Years,* 1980, *3*(10), 12–13, 22.

Rosenberg, M. *Society and the adolescent self-image.* Princeton, N.J.: Princeton University Press, 1965.

Rosenberg, M. *Conceiving the self.* New York: Basic Book, 1979.

Rossiter, C. M. H. Chronological age and listening of adult students. *Adult Education Journal,* 1970, *21*(1), 40–43.

Rossman, M. H. *Adult basic education: A manual for teachers in Arizona.* Tempe: Arizona State University, 1977.

Ryan, T. F. Analyzing the questioning activity of students and teachers. *College Student Journal,* 1972, *6*(2), 116–21.

Ryan, T. A., & Furlong, W. Literacy program in industry, the armed forces and penal institutions. In J. B. Carroll & J. S. Chall (Eds.), *Toward a literate society.* New York: McGraw Hill, 1977.

Sainz, J. A., & Biggins, M. G. *Effective methodology for teaching beginning reading in English to bilingual adults.* 1980. (ERIC Document Reproduction Service No. ED 190 983)

Sanders, N. *Classroom questions: What kinds?* New York: Harper & Row, 1966.

Satlow, I. D. 120 questions about your questioning technique. *Business Education World,* 1969, *4*(6), 20–22.

Scales, A. M., & Biggs, S. A. *Reading for illiterates and semiliterate adults: An assessment-prescriptive instructional model.* Paper presented at the Annual Reading Conference of the St. Thomas Reading Council, St. Thomas, March 1976. (ERIC Document Reproduction Service No. ED 126 500)

Schaie, K. W. Rigidity-flexibility and intelligence: A cross-sectional study of the adult life-span from 20 to 70. *Psychological Monographs.* 1948, *72*(9).

Schaie, K. W. External validity in the assessment of intellectual development in adulthood. *Journal of Gerontology,* 1978, *33,* 695–701.

Schaie, K. W., & Parr, J. Intelligence. In A. W. Chickering and Associates (Eds.), *The modern American college: Responding to the new realities of diverse students and a changing society.* San Francisco: Jossey-Bass, 1981.

Schaie, K. W., & Willis, S. L. Life-span development: Implications for education. In L. S. Shulman (Ed.), *Review of research in education.* Ithaca, Ill.: Peacock, 1979.

Seels, B., & Dale, E. Readability and reading. An annotated bibliography, 1971 revision. (ERIC Document Reproduction Service No. ED 075 789)

Servey, R. E. *Teacher talk: The knack of asking questions.* Belmont, Cal.: Fearon, 1974.

Sharon, A. T. Adult academic achievement in relation to formal education and age. *Adult Education,* 1971, *21*(4), 231–37.

Sheehy, G. *Passages: Predictable crises of adult life.* New York: E. P. Dutton & Co., 1976.

Sheffield, S. B. The orientations of adult continuing learners. In Daniel Solomon (Ed.), *The continuing learner.* Chicago: Center for the Study of Liberal Education for Adults, 1964.

Sherman, D. C., & Buchanan, B. M. *Adult readers and the texts they need or want to read.* 1980. (ERIC Document Reproduction Service No. ED 197 302)

Silber, E., & Tippett, J. S. Self-esteem: Clinical assessment and measurement validation. *Psychological Report,* 1965, *16,* 1017–71.

Sjogren, D. D., Knox, A. B., & Grotelueschen, A. Adult learning in relation to prior adult education participation. *Adult Education Journal,* 1968, *19*(1), 3–10.

Smith, C. R. The relationship between self-concept and success in the freshman year of college. *New Outlook for the Blind,* 1972, *66,* 84–89.

Smith, D. H. The development of a comprehensive information system for assessing the progress and follow-up service of ABE students and former students. Des Moines: Iowa State Department of Public Instruction, final report for FY 1980, Project No. 04, 1980. (ERIC Document Reproduction Service No. ED 192 069)

Sorenson, H. Adult ages as a factor in learning. *Journal of Educational Psychology,* 1930, *21,* 451–59.

Stovall, T. F. Lecture vs. discussion. *Phi Delta Kappan,* 1958, *39*(6), 255–58.

Strong, E. K. *Changes of interest with ages.* Palo Alto, Ca.: Stanford University Press, 1953.

Struck, J. W. How to question students effectively. *Industrial Arts and Vocational Education,* 1962, *51,* 26–27.

Suessmuth, P. R., & Stengels, M. Warm them up, ask the right questions. *Training in Business and Industry,* 1972, *9*(5), 33–36.

Sund, R. B. Through sensitive listening and questioning. *Childhood Education,* 1974, *51,* 68–71.

Sund, R. B. *Creative questioning and sensitive listening techniques: A self-concept approach* (2nd ed.). Columbus, Oh.: C. E. Merrill, 1978.

Taba, H. The teaching of thinking. *Elementary English,* 1965, *42*(5), 534–42.

Taylor, S. *A reference source of tests and other evaluation instruments for public school adult education.* Bulletin No. 7H1-7. Tallahassee: Department of Education, 1974.

Teft, S. On-the-job training now includes classes to boost literacy. *Chicago Tribune,* February 15, 1982, p. 9.

Thompson, R. Learning to question. *Journal of Higher Education,* 1969, *40*(6), 467–72.

Thorndike, E. L. *Adult interests.* New York: Macmillan, 1935.

Thorndike, E. L., Bergman, E. O., Tilton, W. J., & Woodyard, E. *Adult Learning.* New York: Macmillan, 1928.

Traver, J. L. Adult learning: You can't teach an old dog new tricks. *Training and Development Journal,* 1975, *29,* 44–47.

Vanderhaar, K., Mocker, D. W., Leikert, R. E., & Moass, V. *Tests for adult basic education teachers.* Kansas City: University of Missouri School of Education, Center for Resource Development in Adult Education, 1975.

Verduin, J. R., Miller, H. G., & Green, C. E. *Adults teaching adults.* Austin, Tex.: Learning Concepts, 1977.

Verner, C., & Davison, C. *Psychological factors in adult learning and education* (Research to Practice Series). Tallahassee: Florida State University, 1971.

Wallach, M. A., & Green, L. R. On age and the subjective speed of time. *Journal of Gerontology,* 1961, *16*(1), 71–74.

Walmsley, S. A. Effects of document simplificating on the reading comprehension of the elderly. *Journal of Reading,* 1981, *13*(3), 237–48.

Warren, V. B. *How adults can learn more—faster.* Washington, D.C.: National Association of Public School Adult Educators, 1961.

Wechsler, D. *The measurement of adult intelligence* (Rev. ed.). Baltimore: Williams & Wilkins, 1955.

Weiss, A. D. Sensory functions. In J. E. Birren (Ed.), *Handbook of aging and the individual.* Chicago: University of Chicago Press, 1959.

Wellington, J. What is a question. *Education Digest,* 1962, *28,* 38–39.

Wells, L. E., & Maxwell, G. *Self-esteem: Its conceptualization and measurement.* Beverly Hills, Cal.: Sage, 1976.

Whipple, J. B. *Especially for adults*. Boston: Center for the Study of Liberal Education for Adults, 1957.

Williams, A. R., et al. *Readability of textual materials—a survey of the literature*, 1974. (ERIC Document Reproduction Service No. ED 097 642)

Woodruff, D. S., & Walsh, D. A. Research in adult learning: The individual. *The Gerontologist*, 1975, *15*, 424–30.

Wyatt, S. *In-service staff development: A basic content reading curriculum for ABE teaching personnel*. Salt Lake City: Utah State Board of Education, 1980. (ERIC Document Reproduction Service No. ED 192 122)

Zahn, J. C. Differences between adults and youth affecting learning. *Adult Education*, 1967, *17*(2), 67–77.

Zahn, J. C. Some adult attitudes affecting learning: Powerlessness, conflicting needs and role transition. *Adult Education*, 1969, *19*(2), 91–97.

Zahorik, J. A. Questioning in the classroom. *Education*, 1971, *91*(4), 358–63.

Zimmerman, B. J., & Bergan, J. R. Intellectual operations in teacher questioning-asking behavior. *Merrill Palmer Quarterly of Behavior and Development*, 1971, *17*(1), 19–26.

INDEX